What's Your LipStory?

An Illustrated Guide to Understanding the Messages in Your Lip Prints

Pam Fox

What's Your LipStory?
An Illustrated Guide to Understanding the Messages in Your Lip Prints
by Pamela Fox

Copyright © 2015 by Pamela Fox

ISBN: 978-0-692-48724-2

All rights reserved. No part of this book may be reproduced by any mechanical, photographic, or electronic process, or in the form of an audio recording, nor may it be stored in a retrieval system, transmitted or otherwise be copied for public or private use, other than for "fair use" as brief quotations embodied in articles and reviews, without prior written permission of the copyright owner.

Disclaimer and Informed Consent:

The interpretation tools, techniques, processes and protocols described in *What's Your LipStory? – An Illustrated Guide to Understanding the Messages in Your Lip Prints* are for informational and educational purposes only. They are not intended to diagnose, prescribe, treat, or cure any disease or mental condition.

In addition, the interpretation techniques described in this book are not intended as a substitute for professional care. No action or inaction should be taken based solely on the contents herein; instead readers or participants should consult appropriate health professionals on any matter relating to their mental or physical health. The FDA has not evaluated this information and there are no curative claims. The author shall have no liability or responsibility to any individual or entity for any alleged loss or damage caused by the use or misuse of the information in this book.

The author will, however, take at least partial responsibility for the enjoyment and inspiration experienced by readers of this material!

Using the interpretation techniques herein is acknowledgment that you have read, understand, and agree to this disclaimer and therefore that informed consent has been established.

Published by Magic Speaks Publishing

First Printing 2015

Design and graphics by One Voice Can Graphics, Books and Mandalas: www.onevoicecan.com

Photography by Harley Bonham: www.harleybonham.com

For Jim, my steady hand and Strong Willow,

And for Linda, my sister in Spirit, who flew with me to inner and outer spaces.

ACKNOWLEDGMENTS

Notwithstanding the solitary hours, days, months and years that writing a book may involve, it is always a group endeavor. This book would never have come into existence without two very important people in my life. I am ever grateful to Jilly Eddy, the brilliant and intuitive woman who cracked the code for interpreting the messages in our lip prints. Without her willingness to share her knowledge, without her hours of patient instruction and her enthusiastic support, this rich and fulfilling journey that I am on may not have unfolded before me. With all of my heart I say thank you, Jilly!

Equally important to the creation process has been the cheerleading and coaching of my husband, Jim. It is he who introduced me to Jilly, who encouraged me to leave a more traditional career path and to follow my heart and intuition as I learned to read lip prints. Jim, your unflagging belief in me and in the wisdom of our lips has carried me through the inevitable fits and starts of exploring a new life path. For your love, comfort, patience, support, and eternal optimism, I am deeply thankful.

There are many others who have contributed to the fulfillment of the dream I've held of writing this book. From the teachings of the Deer Tribe I received wisdom teachings and a beautiful way of expressing that knowledge. I especially extend my gratitude to my Red Lodge teacher, Razel Wolf (Singing Otter Woman). With your piercing discernment and guidance, your playfulness and humor, your poetic fluidity of articulation and your ironclad commitment to honoring the ceremony of life, you've been a powerful image-maker for me as I have grown into my medicine name.

To KC Miller, the quintessential Diamond Girl, your beauty, passion and unflagging movement forward, bringing all in your wake along with you, I say thank you for your support.

Over the course of the several years it took to complete this book, I have benefited from the editorial advice of three people. Caren Cantrell, my original editor, helped me begin the process of refining the book. Lisa Forner was the catalyst who moved me out of inertia several months later. Finally, the talented and insightful Michelle Radomski and her husband Joe led me out of the formatting wilderness I was lost in! The book would not have come into completion in such a beautiful and coherent way without their help. Thanks to all of you.

And to my sweet sister, Sandy, her husband, their children and grandchildren, my aunts, uncles and cousins, and my "other mother" Ruth: you have all inspired me, in each of your ways, to soften to myself and others, to love without condition and to aspire to living a conscious, mindful life. Thank you all for being my safe harbor.

My friends (you know who you are) have cheered me on and kept me motivated. We've talked about the teachings in this amazing new modality and we've ruminated and mulled over the sometimes complex and confusing implications and clues to understanding the meaning of this or that. You have been my brain trust and my sounding board. I love you all more than I can say.

To the countless friends, family, clients and guests who have turned over their most private inner workings to me in the form of a lip print: I appreciate your trust. I have learned something from each of you. With this book I say thank you for all that you contributed to my understanding of the Universal Truths that can be found in a simple waxy smudge on paper.

There are several people who granted me permission to use their names and stories in this book. The book would be poorer without their inclusion and I am grateful for the faith they have in me. I hope I have served you all well.

I especially want to thank two more people. My beautiful niece, Teri, whose snappy clarity is combined with the sagacity of an elder living in the body of a 40-something yoga teacher: Your observations have always been more helpful than you know, but even more, who you are being as a mother, wife, daughter, teacher, friend and Sacred Human Being has inspired me to continue seeking a higher vibration for myself. Thank you for growing up to be my friend!

And finally, I am grateful to my mother, Willie. I have been blessed with a mother who loves me unconditionally, who will stand for me, praise me, defend me, pray for me, motivate me, worry about me, who has been there from the beginning and will be there until her last day, and mine. You are and always will be the Angel on my shoulder. Thank you for your devotion and unwavering belief that all good things are possible in life, Mom. I love you.

FOREWORD
BY JILLY EDDY

Intrigued by what I was doing, Pam Fox called me in 2008 and asked if I would agree to teach her Lipsology™, the art and science of reading lip prints. I said, "Yes!" Over the next several months, I taught her what I have discovered about how our lip prints reveal information regarding our personalities, energy levels, emotions, and health indicators.

She took to reading lip prints like a duck to water! Lip prints speak to her. She listens. She accurately, uncannily, uses her lip print reading knowledge to make a positive difference in the lives of many people.

I think Pam's book is brilliant! In it she speaks wisdom, offering gentle guidance and profound insights. She skillfully weaves what she learned from me into her own new lip print discoveries. I found myself highlighting many wonderful, inspiring paragraphs for later contemplation and study. After reading the book twice, there are sections I want to come back to and study; digest more carefully.

She makes me proud to say I am her teacher. She has become an expert in her own right … a teacher of teachers!

Pam has included many new ideas and discoveries—which totally intrigue me and have me looking at the examples and interpretations with an eye to watching for them. I feel as excited as a little kid in a candy shop to try them out and see how "right on" they prove to be! Brava, Pam!

Whether you are a seasoned Certified Lipsologist, a new student of Lipsology™, or a person interested in reading about a fascinating subject, you will find Pam Fox's book a wonderful resource and enjoyable read.

So put on some lipstick and kiss some paper—I assure you, you will see yourself in these pages and be amazed at what your lip prints have to say about you!

Jilly Eddy - Founder of Lipsology™

A NOTE FROM THE AUTHOR

When I began writing this book, my intention was to write about Lip Print Reading in a way that would make this new modality easily accessible to the general public. However, as I progressed, I found myself writing a more comprehensive book than I had planned, ultimately sharing all that I currently know about this intriguing subject. The result is a textbook that is suitable for the serious student of Lipsology™.

Still, the book is also user-friendly enough to be used by the casual reader who simply wants to track the messages embedded in her own lip prints. Whether you choose to study the book cover to cover or just flip through it finding the indicators that apply to you, I am certain that you will be surprised and inspired by the information you'll discover in your lip prints. And I hope that you will find, as I have, that Lip Print Reading is an exciting and dynamic new way to open a portal to self-awareness and presence. It has transformed my life, and, dear reader, I am certain that it can do the same for you.

TABLE OF CONTENTS

Acknowledgments 5
Foreword 7
A Note from the Author 9
Table of Contents 11
A Brief History of Lip Print Reading 15
Let's Begin 21
Frequently Asked Questions 25

Part 1: The Personality Indicators 33
A Map of the Lips 35
Size Matters! 37
    The Large Lip Print 38
    The Medium Lip Print 39
    The Small Lip Print 40
The Meaning Of Shapes 43
    Round and Oval 46
    Square and Rectangle 50
    Triangle 54
    Diamond 58
    Irregular 61
    Hybrid 66
    Shapes Shape Your Life 68
Clarity 69
Fullness 71
Position 81
    Charting the Position of a Print 83
Spacing 85

The Significance of Corners 91
    Corner Spacing 92
    Information Funnels 98
    Information Eddy 101
    Zingers 102
    I've Got a Secret! 104
    Blinders 105
    Happy or Droopy? 107
    Bff ~ Best Friends Forever 109

Important Features of the Upper Lip 111
    Cupid's Bow 111
    Smooth~Top 113
    People Movers 115
    The Hug Pucker 117
    The Mother Hen 121

Important Features Of The Lower Lip 123
    Lower Cupid's Bow 123
    Personal Pusher 125
    Pointed Bottom 126
    Round Bottom 127
    Center Stage 127
    The Gourmet Lip Split 129
    Multiple Gourmet Lip Split 131
    Lower Hug Pucker 132

General Color Intensity 133

Part 2: The Energetic Indicators 137

Essence and Energy 139

The Physical Indicators 145
    Intensity and Fading 145
    Non-Physical Fading 148
    Inner Reserves 150
    Peppering 151
    Lower Peppering 151
    Missing Parts vs. Asymmetry 152
    Lip Anatomy Map 154

Mental Indicators 157
    Mental Memos 159
    Mental Memos in the Hug Pucker 161
    White Noise 161
    Stress (is Always a Choice!) 163
    Stress in the Hug Pucker 165
    Upper Peppering 166
    Lines of Concern.. 167
    Worry, Regret and Distraction 168
    Gale Marks... 172
    Worry And Gale Marks in the GLS 174

Emotional Indicators 177
    Emotional Mottling.. 177
    Challenge Line 178
    Journey Line 180
    Faded Apex 183
    Communication Gap 185
    Tipsy Lip Prints.. 188
    Line of Overwhelm 189

Spiritual Indicators 191
    Spiritual Receptors... 191
    Angel Marks.. 192
    The Hand of God 193
    Lines of Intuition 194
    Psychic Wedges... 195
    Angel Wings.. 196
    Helping Hands 198
    Seeds of Transformation 199
    Starburst... 200
    Angel Dust and Intuitive Mist... 202

Passionate/Creative Indicators... 205
    Passion 206
    Creativity... 206
    Dancing Lip Prints 208
    Symbols.. 211

Combining Indicators.. 215

Sample Reading 217
In Conclusion 227
About the Author 229
Endnotes 231
Bibliography 233
Glossary 235
Index 241

A BRIEF HISTORY OF LIP PRINT READING

Lipstick

Four thousand five hundred years ago, a Sumerian noblewoman, known as Queen Puabi,[i] lived, ruled, and died in the city of Ur in ancient Mesopotamia, modern-day Iraq. In 1920 her body was found in a royal tomb along with the remains of five soldiers, two oxen and their four grooms, plus seventeen ladies-in-waiting, all sacrificed to be of service to the Queen in the afterlife.

Along with her elaborate golden headdress and jewelry, a cape made of strands of lapis lazuli and carnelian beads, rings on every finger, and a gold and jeweled diadem, there were furniture, an exquisite gold and lapis lyre, a sled, textiles and a multitude of golden ornaments and vessels. Among all of these precious artifacts, archeologists also found cosmetics which would have been used for adorning the eyes and lips. It seems that forty-five hundred years ago a Sumerian noblewoman valued "lipstick" enough to be buried with it!

Some anthropologists believe that humans have been decorating their faces and bodies ritualistically for over 100,000 years, since the Paleolithic age. Makeup, including lipstick or its equivalent, has been around for a very long time.

Over thousands of years, lipstick has been made from a wide variety of ingredients. Queen Puabi's lip color would have been made from crushed gemstones or iron rich minerals and, possibly lead, which is toxic. From the days of the Greeks, Romans, and Egyptians to the last years of Victorian England, women have blended ingredients such as red ochre, red wine, mulberries and seaweed, gum Arabic, egg whites, and fig milk into tinted lip balms. First Lady Martha Washington used a recipe including beeswax, lard, sugar, almond oil, alkanet (a plant based red dye), raisins, and balsam.

In 2012 it was disclosed that Starbucks was using cochineal, a red coloring made from dried insects, to color their Strawberry Frappuccino®. Some customers were disturbed by this at the time. Yet the same crushed bugs have been tinting lip color for centuries.[ii]

Today, unless you buy lipstick that is stamped USDA Organic or certified by the Natural Products Association, you may be applying lipstick that is made from rendered animal fat, tissue and body parts, as well as pigments, fish scales, wax, and oil, not so different from what Mrs. Washington concocted. However, you may also be using a product that contains formaldehyde, coal tar, benzene, nitrosamines, talc and even lead, ingredients that can be dangerous to your health. In a study done by the European Scientific Commission on Consumer Safety, over a lifetime, the average woman may ingest close to 4 pounds of lipstick.[iii] If you have concerns about what you are wearing and eating, check your labels!

Lip Prints and Crime

Fans of any of the popular crime lab shows on TV may like to say "thank you" to a French criminologist named Edmond Locard.[iv] Dubbed the "French Sherlock Holmes," he opened the very first crime lab in Lyon, France in 1910. Locard, a student of both medicine and law, was interested in discovering all that he could about what he called the "trace evidence" left behind and carried away from the scene of a crime. He came up with the underlying principle of forensic science, that "every contact leaves a trace." In his laboratory, he studied footprints, fingerprints, lip prints, hair and thread samples, and anything that might lead an investigator to understand what had happened at a crime scene, and more importantly, who was there when it happened. Locard's interest in lip prints was purely for forensic purposes.

The work of Edmond Locard preceded extensive studies done by Japanese and Indian researchers beginning in 1950. Two of those scientists, Yasuo Suchhihashi and Kazuo Suzuki, examined 1,364 persons at the department of forensic odontology at Tokyo University from 1968 to 1971.[v] They established that the arrangement of lines on the red part of the human lips is individual and unique for each human being. This kind of study of lip prints would come to be called cheiloscopy. Their studies do not seem to have included the other features of a lip print, such as the fullness, shape, and size but instead focused on the uniquely individual furrows that each lip print presents. If a print is not of high enough quality to distinguish these almost microscopic lines, the forensic value of the print is diminished.

Ironically, nowadays with modern technology it's possible to identify the owner of a print with a simple DNA sample taken from the area of the print, making the quality of the print less important than the presence of it.

All of these early studies of the nature and qualities of lip prints had nothing to do with classic physiognomy, or with what we will learn about in this book. The goal of these past studies was to find a way to identify the owner of a lip print using individually unique identifiers, like the ones we have in our fingerprints. To a certain extent the research succeeded, but our lip prints have much more to reveal to us than "who done it!"

Physiognomy

Physiognomy literally means the overall outer physical characteristics of a person. It can refer specifically to face reading, but it is also a general term that includes any method by which you study a part of the person to understand the whole person, and the outside of the person to learn about the inner person.

Face Reading, a form of physiognomy, evolved around 300 BC out of traditional Chinese medicine and acupuncture. Originally face reading was practiced by Taoist monks and scholars, who were part counselor, part priest, part doctor. Chinese practitioners believed then and now, that the features of the face and head could tell the story of a person's health, character, personality and future.

On the subcontinent of India, palmistry, another physiognomic art, began to flourish around the same time that the Chinese were exploring face reading. Although historical details have been lost in the mists of time, it is widely believed that palm reading spread from India to China and from there to Tibet, Japan, Mongolia, Persia, Egypt, and Greece. Ancient cultures were mesmerized by the intriguing possibility of finding the answers to life's questions literally at their fingertips, mapped out on their very bodies!

Over the centuries, the arts of palm reading, face reading, and personology (reading the whole body) spread around the civilized world. Unfortunately, these practices were often perverted by shysters and crooks, posing as fortune tellers, resulting in plenty of bad press. King Henry the VIII outlawed palmistry. The church called all forms of fortune telling a sin, and still teaches so today.

But a true practitioner of any physiognomic modality is not in the business of telling fortunes. Remember that face reading comes out of the time-honored traditions of Chinese medicine. The Chinese recognized early that to the degree that the mind shapes the body, we can take heed of what is being transmitted and use that information to move ourselves toward our goals. Modern hand readers base their readings on 20th century research that has validated much of what was originally intuited by the East Indians. Technology has shown us that the body responds to thoughts and feelings and the responses can be seen and measured. There is indeed communication between the inner realm of being and the outer realm of the physical. If we are wise, we can learn how to understand and benefit from what is being expressed.

A Convergence

Okay. Lipstick, or its equivalent, has been around for thousands of years. The study of messages on body parts has been around for at least 2500 years. In the last century, there has been interest in the study of lip prints, but when and where did lip prints, lipstick and physiognomy finally collide and coalesce into what we now call Lip Print Reading, the understanding of the micro-expressions of the lips?

I'm glad that you asked!

In my research I have found no recorded evidence that anyone put lip prints, lipstick, and physiognomy together in a way that was as accurate and compelling as Jilly Eddy did in 1990.

It began in 1981 when Jilly bought the book, *With Love From . . . .*[vi] The book is a collection of lip prints of famous people and was sold as a fund raiser for the Save the Children Fund.

Inspired by the book, Jilly, who was living in Bellingham, Washington at the time, began collecting lip prints as a hobby, and for 9 years her collection grew to thousands of prints. After an interview in the *Chicago Tribune* brought her and her collection into the public eye, a producer from the *Tonight Show* with Johnny Carson called and asked her to come on the program to talk about famous lip prints she had in her collection. When she admitted that she only had a couple of "famous lip prints," the producer asked her if maybe she could come on the show and talk about the meaning of lip prints. Although Jilly had previously been exploring the possible meaning of lip prints, she didn't feel ready to appear on the show as an authority on the subject. The call from the producer did, however, serve to catalyze Jilly's interest in discovering what our lip prints say about us.

Based on her extensive collection of the prints of friends and family, Jilly began to categorize her collection by size, shape, fullness, placement, color intensity, and so forth. She compared lip prints with what she knew about the people they belonged to, and with what she knew about other physiognomic modalities. Her knowledge of face reading, hand reading, and hand writing analysis revealed clues that led her to a new understanding of the indicators she discovered. She interviewed people who shared the same distinctive features or "indicators" until she began to see what common trait or characteristic they all had. Over time, Jilly isolated 25 indicators, with about one hundred variations, that can display in lip prints. Her research showed that these indicators always mean the same thing in every lip print. She had discovered a universal language of the lips, and she called it Lipsology™.[vii]

What Jilly has discovered about our lip prints since 1990 is impressive. No one else has cracked the code quite as completely as she has. I think of Jilly as the "Rosetta Stone" of lip prints, the human decoder who has deciphered a previously unreadable language. Although I believe there is still much more to learn about the messages in our lip prints, Jilly has given us plenty of territory to explore.

In 2008 I heard about Jilly's work. I had recently begun to work as a hand reader at parties and corporate events, and I was fascinated by the idea of reading a lip print. I called Jilly and asked her if she would teach me what she knew. Happily, she agreed to do so! By late 2008 I was reading prints professionally, and it has become my passion. The more I learn about this technique of lip print reading, the more admiration and respect I feel for Jilly and the body of work that she has brought into being.

Occasionally I have made adjustments or additions to her teachings based on client feedback and my own observations. I liken it to going to culinary school to learn the basics of French Cooking. All western cuisines are based on the French formula and if you know French cooking, you can use it as a basis for almost any other style of food you care to play with. In a similar way, Jilly's foundation of Lipsology™ is the baseline for interpreting lip prints. It is where I start in any reading. I have added my own flavorings and seasonings in the interpretation of certain indicators and features, and I have discovered a new "dish" or two on my own. Lip Print Reading is a nascent and evolving technique for self-reflection, presence and personal development. As you learn to read your own lip prints and those of others, I'm certain that you too will find reason to honor Jilly's discoveries.

LET'S BEGIN

Now is a good time to make your first **Kiss Card**. Begin collecting your own lip prints, and ask others for theirs. The more lip prints you collect, the more understanding you'll have of how this works.

How to Make a Kiss Card

- Fold a blank piece of paper or card stock in half and cut into two 5½ x 8½ inch pieces (This is a Kiss Card!)

- Have a pen handy.

- Use a dark, matte, non-frosted lipstick

- Before making your prints, wipe your lips with a tissue to remove any lipstick, gloss, or cream that may be there.

- Apply the lipstick yourself. It's best if everyone applies his/her own lipstick.

- Make at least three prints on the paper so that you have a nice sampling to look at. Number the order of the prints.

- Write your name and the date on the bottom of the page.

Now you have your first set of prints.

Begin asking people you know if they will help you learn how to read lip prints by giving you a set of their prints. You'll want to always have a "lip-kit" close at hand stocked with:

- An unopened lipstick

- A small mirror

- Some tissues

- A few Kiss Cards

Have your subjects follow the instructions for "How to Make a Kiss Card." Some people (men and boys usually) will want you to apply the lipstick for them. Encourage them to apply their own. Some may ask you how to make the prints and where to kiss the card. The less instruction you give, the better. This is their message and if the reader or anyone else gives instructions, it isn't completely theirs anymore. I am careful to say, "Make three prints anywhere in the white space, versus "kiss the card 3 times." "Making a print" is not as specific as "kissing." Leave room for their own interpretation.

As you begin to collect prints from any willing subject, consider how you will store your collection. There are lots of options. Just find one that will work for you.

Here are Some Ideas

- Buy a journal for your own lip prints and note the date, how you were feeling and what was going on in your day with each entry of prints. If you already journal daily, just add your lip prints to your entries.

- Store the kiss cards you collect from your friends, family and any willing volunteers in file boxes, baskets, or loose leaf 3 ring binders.

- Scan your Kiss Cards and keep them in a file on your computer, but keep the originals.

- Organize your collection by groups like family and friends, by dates, by events, or by features and indicators.

- Begin to notice the variations you see in size, shape, fullness, openness, color intensity and any other observations that come to you.

LET'S BEGIN | 23

FREQUENTLY ASKED QUESTIONS

What kind of information can you see in a lip print?

First we explore the personality of the subject. We look at the features and indicators that describe the way a person interacts and communicates with others. We look at her talents, skills and propensities. We see how she is perceived and how she may perceive herself. This part of the reading may simply affirm what the person already knows, in which case she will at the least be entertained. On the other hand, she may hear the validation she needs to believe in herself and her abilities in ways that she has not been able to until now.

Once we have covered the personality indicators, we move on to part two; the energetic reading.

The energetic reading includes a close look at the energy systems that we all have: those of the physical, the mental, the emotional, the spiritual and the passionate/creative. This part of the reading can be quite inspirational, and sometimes even transformational.

I believe unconditionally in the accuracy of the messages being displayed in our lip prints. Of course, as in any other type of reading, inaccuracies may arise out of a lack of knowledge or skill on the part of the reader, but not in the information that is displayed.

What is the difference between a feature and an indicator?

In general, a feature is the more obvious physical form of a person's lips, such as the size, shape, fullness, the Cupid's Bow, and the Hug Pucker. Indicators are all about the person's qualities and energies and usually cannot be seen without a lip print. Examples are color intensity, stress marks, Zingers, Angel Marks and Psychic Wedges. A feature, like size, can also be an indicator. So you may physically have a large mouth, but in some instances you may make a small lip print, which indicates a personality trait.

Where does the information come from?

It has been said that the mind informs the body. In her book *Toe Reading; Are You Walking Your Destined Path?*[viii] author K.C. Miller writes that our feet, and especially our toes, are micro-representations of the lives we are living.

In a similar way, our faces carry the story of a life lived. A lifetime of worry will leave its marks on one's face, most noticeably between the eyebrows and around the mouth. Crow's feet, laugh lines, marionette lines, and frown lines all tell us something about a life lived. The body responds to our thoughts and emotions in the short term and over time, leaving visible clues as to what's going on in our minds and hearts by sculpting the topography of the body.

In our lip prints this sculpting is rapid and dramatic as our thoughts, emotions, physical energy, connection to spirit, and passions blow through our awareness. Moment by moment our lip prints are recording our disappointments, judgments, confusion, highs, lows and middles. Blood flow and muscle tensions cause contractions that arrange the surface of your lips into patterns that can be deciphered.

Recently I heard about a new MRI that actually shows the flow of thoughts through the brain. Researchers have been able to identify the patterns so accurately, that they can literally read the mind of the person being scanned.[ix] This is what happens on the plains of the lips. Micro-expressions, which appear to be universal, flow across the expanse of the lips like migrating wildebeest, leaving behind evidence of their passage when a lip print is made.

Just as our facial expressions can be read, the indicators in the lips relay information about the state of the person. Unlike our smiles, winks, twitches and frowns, the expressions of our lip prints have gone unnoticed and unappreciated until now. Finally with Jilly's work and our ongoing research, we can tap into this previously hidden wealth of information.

Our lip prints offer a vehicle for stepping out of the ego and into what spiritual teacher Eckhart Tolle calls "spacious awareness." The lips' messages are always benevolent, always a nudge toward greater presence. Although I believe that these messages are a direct physiological expression of our thoughts, feelings, and passions, I also believe that they create the context for spiritual exploration. Each lip print carries the seeds of insight and refinement. Out of our conscious or unconscious connection to the dimension of Infinite Being, the place we turn to in prayer or meditation, we reveal ourselves in our prints, affording each of us a glimpse of a new pathway to wholeness.

Are you a fortune teller?

No. When I read a lip print, I do not read the future. I read the present. As Pulitzer Prize winning author Annie Dillard writes, "How we spend our days is, of course, how we spend our lives," so one could predict a probable future based on the continuation of the present life patterns, beliefs and biases that show in a lip print.

Self-awareness is the first and most crucial step to designing the life we want to have in years to come and to breaking the patterns that constrict us. Your lip prints will, rather relentlessly, reflect back to you over and over again, each area where you need to do the work of self-healing. They do not lie, even when you are lying to yourself. There is no end, ever, to the process of refinement that we are all engaged in . . . not until our final day. That's a marvelous thing when you think about it. There's always some large or small craggy spot where we can continue to polish our rough edges, and there is always a deeper experience of presence within reach.

The motivational speaker, Jim Rohn said, "If you want to have more than you have, you need to become more than you are." But how can you become more than you are unless you know who you are being right now, and what being more than you are would require of you? The indicators in your lip prints will reveal who you are being in this very moment. Then, on the basis of that information, you can redirect your energy and intention toward the "more" of your potentiality.

Do my lip prints change?

The answer is yes. Not only do they change from one print to the next, but they will change over short or long periods of time depending on your present moment experience of life. There will never be another print exactly like the one you just made. Each lip print is one-of-a-kind. As each moment of our life is unique, each message in any moment will be unique. Like clouds drifting by on a summer day, recreating themselves from one moment to the next, the indicators in your lip prints will morph from one print to the next, but they will always be speaking your truth. If the messages seem to repeat themselves often, this will occur out of necessity. Our lip prints, like love letters from our Higher Consciousness, will continue to speak the truth to us until we listen.

What can you tell me about my love life?

Your lip prints are essentially all about your relationships, with yourself, with others and with the world around you. Love is available and present everywhere you turn, in every moment, but the essence of this question is usually "What can you tell me about my next or current lover?"

In the very core or heart of the lip print we find the Hug Pucker (1) and the Gourmet Lip Split (2). I call this core area the Circle of Romance. These two indicators hold the most personal information about how you feel, think and communicate in your closest relationships, as well as how passionate you may or may not be feeling. We can see what's going on presently and we can also see places where you can adjust your perspective so as to deepen the relationship you are in or to draw into your life the one you want. We cannot, however, foretell the appearance of a tall dark stranger.

Does having lip enhancement change the reading?

No. I often do readings for women who have had lip enhancement. In fact, I have twice worked at corporate events for one of the companies that makes the injectable filler for lips. Almost every woman I read those two evenings had "enhanced" lips. Each of them expressed surprise at how accurate her reading was and each validated the information that I shared with her. The messages of our lips cannot be adulterated apparently, even when we tamper a bit with nature. In any case, fullness is only one of many indicators, most of which would not be affected by lip enhancement.

Can't you just read my lips by looking at me?

This question is usually asked by men who are curious, but don't want to put on lipstick. No, I cannot read a person's lips accurately just by looking at him. Although a few indicators may be evident, the majority of the indicators in your lips can only be seen in a print. Also, a feature that you can see when you look at someone may disappear when the print is made. For example, the V-shape at the top of the lip, called the Cupid's Bow, is often evident on a face, but may disappear when the lips are pressed to the Kiss Card. There are many indicators that are so finely imprinted that you couldn't see them by looking at someone's lips directly. Indicators like color intensity don't show until the lips are pressed to the paper. The lip print freezes everything in place so that it can be examined like a slide under a microscope. Remember, this is the practice of lip PRINT reading, not LIP reading.

Having said that, I have also come to believe that I should not dismiss the appearance of a person's lips. If on observation of the person's lips I see an indicator that does not show in the prints she gives me, I still recognize the essence of the indicator as at least a subliminal expression inherent in the make-up of that individual, similar to the lines on the non-dominant hand in hand reading.

Can my wife, girlfriend, sister, mother, or you apply the lipstick for me?

Men, like women, are curious about what their lips have to say about them. Once a man has resigned himself to the fact that he cannot get a reading without using lipstick he will often try to enlist the help of the nearest woman to apply the lipstick for him.

However, I always suggest that the man put on his own lipstick, and this is how I explain my position: This is your message conveyed to you in real time by a part of you that chooses to communicate in this indirect way. If you allow someone else to participate in making the lip print by applying your lipstick in her own way, the message may not be completely yours.

A couple of years ago I found a book online that was a collection of lip prints, autographs and photos of famous and not-so-famous actresses from the first half of the Twentieth Century.[x] The author of the book was a handwriting analyst who had interpreted the autographs and the lip prints came from the collection of a major Hollywood make-up artist named Clay Campbell.

It is rare to find lip print collections in print, so I was excited to discover and order the book and I waited for its delivery with great anticipation. I thought it might be useful and fun to compare what the graphologist said to what I could see in the prints.

When I opened the book I was surprised to find that all of the lip prints were virtually identical to each other. How did this happen? I wondered. For example, virtually every single lip print had a Cupid's Bow. And the shapes and spacing were almost like a rubber stamp, they were so similar.

It wasn't until I saw a picture of Mr. Campbell at work in the back of the book that I realized, that of course, all of the lip prints had been collected after he had applied the lipstick to each of the actresses. It may be that he then instructed them on how to make the print. This would explain the overwhelming similarity of all the prints.

I have collected thousands of lip prints and of these, less than 25% have Cupid's Bows, and the shapes and spacing are wildly varied. The chance that virtually 100% of the women whose lip prints were in this collection would have Cupid's Bows and be so similar is small unless they were made to look so by design.

It would be wonderful to see the prints they might have made without the help of Mr. Campbell. I'm certain there would have been a great deal more of the variety of their authentic personalities on display.

This is why I suggest that you apply your own lipstick and that you make the print in whatever way feels natural to you. Otherwise, you may create in your prints someone else's message about you and not an authentic representation of who you are in that moment. Having said that, if the only way a man or a child can make a Kiss Card for me is with someone else's help, there's still going to be a story to read in each print.

Once the lipstick is on, I never give explicit directions on how to make the lip print. I want my subjects to be free to express themselves as naturally as possible. Unfettered by my instructions or interference, men, women and children will deliver a set of kisses unique to each of them. My job is to stay out of the way so their individuality can shine through. So, gentlemen, "man up" and put on your lipstick!

One more comment about men and lipstick . . .

I am amazed at the power that a small tube of wax with color in it has to intimidate the male ego. Although there are an encouraging number of men who step up at my events and grab the lipstick with gusto, there are those who back away and look at me as though I am crazy when I ask them to apply lipstick. Are they being triggered by unconscious core beliefs that this little thing, a tube of lipstick, can define them, and not in a "good" way?

Like the cross held high in old vampire movies, a lipstick can strike terror in the hearts of men and drive them in hordes across the room and out of the reach of its power to contaminate their masculinity!

To all of these men I say, there is nothing to fear . . . lipstick is just a tool. It won't hurt or change you. It doesn't mean anything except what you make it mean . . . and it will come off.

And . . . I have just the color for you!

Part 1

The Personality Indicators

A MAP OF THE LIPS

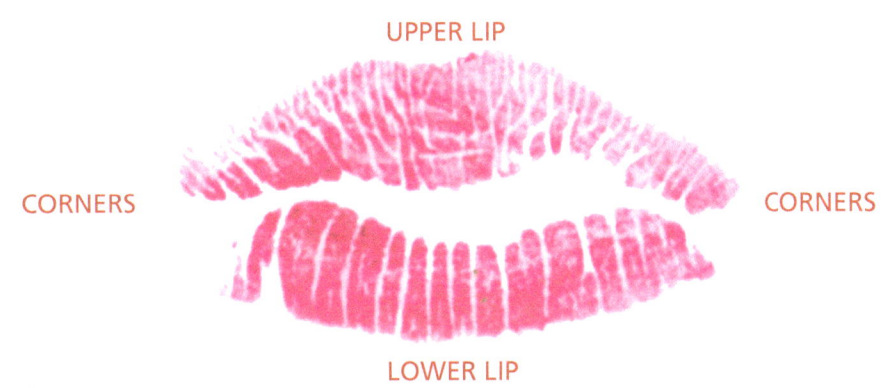

UPPER LIP

CORNERS — CORNERS

LOWER LIP

Locations of Indicators		
UPPER LIP	**CORNERS**	**LOWER LIP**
Your Affectionate Nature	Keeping Secrets	Love of Nature
Response to "Out There"	Response to Change	Judgment of Self
Your Opinion of the Opinion of Others	Presence	Regrets
Autonomy	Decision Making	Appetites and Desires
Leadership Abilities	Information Gathering	Procrastination
Mental Distractions	Wit/Humor	Life Purpose
Physical Vitality	Caution/Control	Communication Skills
Spiritual Receptors	Kindness	Generosity
Communication in Close Relationships	Tact (or lack of)	Worry
Listening Skills	Curiosity	Intuition
	Spontaneity	Physical Health
	Attachments	

The upper and lower lips, as well as the corners of the lips have their own domains. As a general overview, we'll look briefly at what those are, but each aspect will be discussed in detail later.

On the upper lip we find indicators that have to do with the world around us, and our response to it. Here is where we discover how well we listen to others, and how broad a range of subjects we are interested in. We'll see how we lead or avoid leading others, when we are feeling challenged by the behavior of others, and what we think others think of us. When we are excited about our relationships or disappointed in them, when we are distracted by things we need to do, the indicators will be in the upper lip. When we are spiritually engaged or when we are disconnected, when we are lost in our thoughts or feeling stressed by things and events we can't control, our upper lip will tell the tale.

The corners are primarily about caution, change, information, secrets and decision making. They'll tell us about our curiosity, whether we hold on to people, thoughts or things, and how adventurous or easily bored we are.

The lower lip tells us about our outgoing communications, our speaking, writing, and singing. It's here that we demonstrate the extent of our humor, our appetites, our curiosity and our passions. Our ambition and sometimes our life purpose will be evidenced here in specific indicators. When we are troubled or regretful or overly self-critical, it shows here. We'll see in the lower lip whether we are connected to nature and our intuitive guidance, or if hugging a tree might open us up to new insights.

SIZE MATTERS!
WHAT SIZE ARE YOU?

How to Determine the Size of a Lip Print

Print 1: Large Lip Print

Large lips make a print about 2.25 inches wide or wider. Extra height or fullness will add to the characteristics of the size.

Print 2: Medium Lip Print

Medium lips make a print approximately 1.5 to 2.25 inches wide. Prints that are right on the "cusp" of either measurement will share the energy of the adjoining size. A medium size lip print with thin lips will incline toward the characteristics of a small lip print, while full lips will pull in the qualities of a larger lip print.

The height of a lip print will contribute to the overall size, so consider the bulk, or lack of it, when deciding which size category applies.

Print 3: Small Lip Print

Small lip prints are about 1.5 inches or smaller. The thinner the lips the more the characteristics of the small lip print will prevail.

THE LARGE LIP PRINT
Livin' Large!

Lip prints, just like Goldilocks' Bears, come in three sizes: small, medium and large. Your lip print size indicates your world view, where you see yourself fitting into the scheme of things when you are navigating through your tasks, work, or projects and whether you prefer to work alone or with others, behind the scenes or at the helm.

Print 4: Large Lip Print

People with large lip prints have a world view of themselves that includes setting grand goals, doing things in an expansive way and doing them well. Like a hawk circling over a valley keenly watching for the smallest movement of its prey, this size denotes someone who can visualize and manage the big picture while skillfully tracking the details.

This is one indicator that is fairly easy to predict by looking at the person. I will remind you not to assume anything before you see an actual print. Someone with large lips may give you a small or thin lip print. However, for illustration purposes, it might be fun to give you some notion of who would be a good example of the large lip print.

First, you don't have to be a large person to have large lip prints. Lip size has little to do with your height, weight, race, age, or gender.

Kentucky Derby winning jockey, Mike Smith is 5'4" and weighs 114 pounds, and yet he has a large smile and would likely have a large lip print. He has won over 5000 horse races. Picture Mick Jagger performing on stage, Jim Carey in *Pet Detective*, and Oprah Winfrey announcing she is taking her audience to Australia. These people are good examples of what a large lip print looks like in action.

If the lips are full, the owner will prefer to conceptualize the big picture and delegate the details of the work to others. Thin lips or thin corners will suggest someone who prefers to personally oversee every detail.

Other "Livin' Large" personalities might include basketball great Michael Jordan, movie producer and director Steven Spielberg, Grammy winner Lady Gaga, and

Google CEO Larry Page. Stephen Hawking is an excellent example of what it means to express as a large lip print.

Large lip print people like to play with the big boys. They don't want their dreams to be inhibited by anyone else's lack of vision, limited budget or time-stamped schedule. Like a winning race horse, the large lip print would prefer to be given his head and allowed to run for the finish line at his most efficient pace with all of the visionary gusto he has at his disposal.

Are you the owner of a pair of large lips? When you are "living your size" you have the ability to overcome the naysayers around you and to lead the charge toward whatever goal you decide to capture. You are the fearless warrior, a proverbial King Arthur who knows that a big vision can be accomplished and who finds the means to do so in the process of fulfilling your dreams.

THE MEDIUM LIP PRINT
The Happy Medium

Look up "medium" in any dictionary and you'll find several definitions. Here are three:

1. An average state or condition existing between two extremes: the happy medium.

2. The material or environment in which an organism lives.

3. Materials that artists use.

Print 5: Medium Lip Print

There is nothing that implies average about having a medium-sized lip print. As a Happy Medium, you are always doing a balancing act, trying to find the most harmonious combination of directed attention to each area of your life. You are a blend of the big picture person and the detail manager, and your life will feel sometimes like a never-ending race to get this thing organized and that thing done. Between your responsibilities to your family, work or school, spiritual and social lives, things you need to do at home, in your yard, to your car, and the busy scheduling needed to track it all, you may often feel like a juggler trying to keep a dozen bowling pins in the air all at once. Doing so without getting beaned in the process can sometimes take super-human skills! No Ma'am! There is nothing average about the Happy Medium.

Medium-sized lip print owners have great multitasking instincts. I heard of a study recently that claimed that multitasking is a myth, that the notion of having your attention on more than one action at a time is not true or possible. It may be semantics (we do get lost in our thoughts and go into automatic when driving, for example) but anyone who has watched a mother of two talk on the phone while packing their lunches, feeding them breakfast and getting them dressed and out the door to school might question such a study.

Our Happy Mediums have the potential to do a great job of managing all the details in their lives, but are often in danger of "whelming over," especially if they are also a Problem Solver – more about that in the next chapter.

People who are expressing as Happy Mediums might include former Secretary of State Hillary Clinton, Facebook COO Sheryl Sandberg, and University of California President Janet Napolitano. If you're a Happy Medium, be good to yourself. Whether you are shuttling kids from dance classes to soccer fields, or running an international conglomerate, find time during your day to reboot and relax. Remember, you are the person keeping things in balance. You are, for those who depend on you, the "medium" in which they thrive. Prepare to co-create your life and theirs as a work of art.

THE SMALL LIP PRINT
God is in the Details...

In *Goldilocks and the Three Bears*, Goldilocks, evidently a very precocious child, walks uninvited into the home of the Three Bears. Seeing their table set with food, she samples all three bowls and eats all of Baby Bear's porridge. She also finds that it is Baby Bear's chair and bed that suit her best. This was no surprise to me when I first heard the story as a child. Baby Bear had child-friendly accouterments most suited to a little girl like Goldilocks.

What we learned as children in the story of Goldilocks is that one size does not fit all. As adults we know that the world is a better place for our differences and for the special gifts that each of us can offer to those for whom they are a fit.

So thank heavens for all of you with a small lip print!

Print 6: Small Lip Print

You are the detail people. If you have a small lip print, it is likely that you are either very organized, or that you have an almost obsessive desire to be more organized than you are. You are likely to take things literally and to have high expectations of others. Your attention to the minutest detail of any project and your ability to laser in on every component's sequence and place in the greater whole make you invaluable to the success of any project. Some of you Baby Bears will deny that you are organized, but if you think about it, you'll see at least some circumstances in which you always excel at bringing home the goods ahead of schedule and under budget. Perfectionists abound in this category of lip prints, especially when the upper lip is thin.

In an office situation, we need someone to oversee the big picture and others who can handle lots of tasks at the same time, but equally valuable is the person who can do the accounting, keep the files in order, organize the components of the project, and bring fastidiousness and accuracy to the overall situation.

Let me disabuse you right now of any notion that having a small lip print means you are always in a corner with an adding machine or organizing your spice cabinet alphabetically. That may be your passion, but another small-lipped person might be found running a corporation, albeit in a very micromanaging way; think Donald Trump and former German gold medalist Thomas Bach who is the new head of the International Olympic Committee (IOC).

Whatever the size of your lip prints, you hold the potential for creating success. Your lip print size simply affirms your most effective and authentic way of being with others as you move toward your destiny.

THE MEANING OF SHAPES

The shape of your lip prints, the geometric shape you see when you draw an outline around the print, speaks to how you interact with others, as well as which style of connection and communication most compliments your nature. It is the stand you take in the world, your most authentic outward expression of service to others. As such, your shapes suggest an important component of your pathway to self-actualization. For those of you who appreciate astrology, you could think of your shape as something similar to your Sun sign, in the sense that it is a general description. Later, as we learn and integrate the other indicators, we come to a more complete picture of your abilities, potential and purpose.

Your shape may suggest that you are a natural leader meant for the spotlight, or that you are most effective when you work behind the scenes coaching others. Perhaps you have an instinct for motivating people or you're skilled at finding just the right kind of material support needed to keep the wheels of progress moving in other people's lives. Are you the problem solver in your family? Do you enjoy volunteering or fund raising? Your lip print shape is waiting to guide your awareness, if you will allow it to, toward your most natural "Path of Purpose" in all that you endeavor to achieve.

If you display more than one shape, then you are versatile in how you engage with others. Some people may have all of the five shapes evident in a set of prints. In this case, all of the shapes belong to you and all are a part of your natural way of being, although one or two will be dominant. You are flexible and adaptable and have a full set of social skills available to you in each of your life arenas.

When we are unaware of our natural way of being, we may spend our years in frustration, setting misplaced goals, turning away from leadership and responsibility, withholding our beauty and occasionally offending the people we care about as well as those we don't. Your lip prints are not by any stretch of the imagination your only resource in your quest for self-understanding, but they are a good and valid one and they are right in front of you at a moment's notice!

Once we connect to the power of our shape or shapes, we can choose to use our natural communication abilities with conscious intention. We begin to own our inherent power. If we desire an understanding of our purpose in life, our lip print shapes can offer important clues and give us a solid foundation from which to begin our climb towards a fuller experience of self-expression and personal fulfillment.

When I do an in-depth reading, I like to take 6 to 9 lip prints so that I can see how consistent any one shape is, or how varied the shapes may be.

There are five basic shapes. They are: Round (and Oval), Square (and Rectangular), Diamond, Triangular (upward and downward facing), and Irregular. An Irregular print is difficult to define geometrically.

The 5 basic shapes and their variations

Round/Oval   **Square/Rectangular**   **Diamond**

Upward and downward Triangular

Anything goes with the Irregular

A Hybrid is a mix of two or more shapes. This is a round/square hybrid.

LIPSTORY | 44

Print 7: Round-Square Hybrid

Some lip prints are almost geometrically perfect; a perfect circle, square, triangle or diamond. But a true, perfect geometric shape is rare. Hybrid shapes, lip prints that suggest more than one shape, are more common. (Print 7)

So a print may appear to be round, but have the suggestion of squareness as well. It may have a top half that is square and a bottom that is triangular. In this case the qualities of both shapes pertain to the owner of the lips.

At other times we'll see a distinct shape in one lip print followed by another different distinct shape in the next one. (See Kiss Card Below)

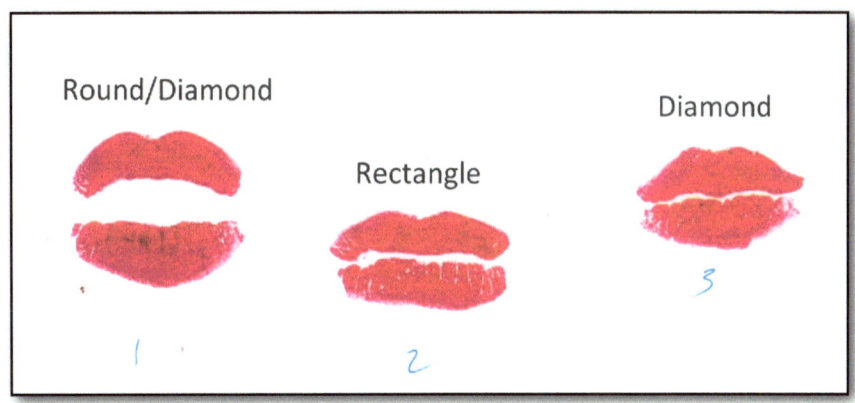

Kiss Card with Varied Shapes

Each shape describes valuable qualities and ways of being. None is superior to another. The world has a need for every one of these expressions, so be proud of your shape and own it with authority!

We will look at the five common shapes of Round, Square, the Triangle, the Diamond and the Irregular. Note that the triangle may be upward or downward pointing, and we will look at the differences implied by this. A round print will mean the same as an oval print and a square print will hold the same qualities as a rectangular print.

After the initial description of each shape's attributes, we'll explore the symbolism of that shape in various cultures and traditions. This additional explanation is offered to you as a way to enhance your perspective and give more context for your readings.

THE MEANING OF SHAPES

Also bear in mind throughout this book that all of the indicators in each lip print come together to give a snapshot of that moment in a person's life experience. We don't want to isolate an indicator and make that be all that the person is. Every indicator blends with the other indicators to form a complex mini-portrait of the person. In astrology, your Sun Sign may be Capricorn, but you also have a Moon Sign, an ascendant, and all of your planets, each influencing the total picture. Likewise, your shape is just one facet to examine and may be enhanced or subdued by any number of other indicators. The final blend will be uniquely YOU!

ROUND AND OVAL
The Provider

We begin with the **Round** and **Oval** lip print. This is the shape of the **Provider**. People with this shape are talented at connecting others to the material resources or tools they need to achieve a common goal. There are two major aspects of the round lip print.

The first is that of the **Accommodating Provider**.

This is the shape of a "people person". In its simplest and perhaps its sweetest expression, this shape indicates someone who cares about the comfort and pleasure of others. She wants everything to run smoothly, like a car with new tires, so that everyone can relax and enjoy life. Like Bobby McFerrin singing, *Don't Worry, Be Happy*, the accommodating aspect of this shape is best displayed in the non-confrontational team player seeking to supply or support comfort, harmony and agreement in all situations.

Accommodating Providers are usually great hosts. If you are invited to the home of this person, your creature comforts will be well attended. You'll eat well, have a comfortable chair, and your host will do everything she can to make sure you have a pleasant evening. Her goal is for you to have a good time and to go home feeling satiated and happy. It gives her joy to know that she did all she could do to bring ease and pleasure to her guests. In the finest articulation of this shape, this desire comes from pure generosity of spirit and a loving nature. She will ask you, "What do you need to be comfortable and happy?"

The second major aspect of this shape is the **Motivating Provider**.

The Motivator aspect is evident in the round lip print with pointed corners protruding from the sides of the circle. (Prints 8 and 9) The points are called "Zingers". The more pronounced the Zingers are, the more intense will be the need to set and achieve goals. Round people with Zingers don't usually see themselves so much as accommodating, or as part of the "Kumbaya" clan! They will rightly identify more with being the real movers and shakers of the "Round People."

Print 8: Round with Zingers

Print 9: Round with Zingers

Very much like a wheel, the round print represents forward movement, going places, and reaching goals and destinations. The owner of this shape motivates others to move toward completion and the desired end result by providing them with the materials, tools or supplies they need, and with verbal prodding. If you are working with this person, she'll be the one asking, "What tools or supplies do you need to get this job done?"

She's the teacher who uses her own paycheck to buy school supplies for her students. She's the volunteer who helps prepare meals for the homeless, or the neighbor who holds a cake sale to raise money for a new women's shelter.

All of these people provide something material that supports the completion or accomplishment of a desired result. The round lip print person lives in the world of supply and demand. He or she is all about supplying what is demanded in the moment.

The round shape owner can hold a grand vision and express on a large scale, especially if the print is large. Habitat for Humanity is a good example of a round expression that has big goals. The Peace Corps and non-profit organizations that respond to natural disasters are all demonstrations of round energy that is "motivated" to provide support. And so is the simple act of feeding you child breakfast and making sure he has a warm coat. On a grand scale or on a smaller scale, round energy moves the world, en masse or one person at a time, towards comfort, security and fulfillment.

The Importance of Being Round

Print 10: Round Lip Print

Used with intention, this shape is an expression of focus, co-creation, achievement and support of the "collective dream." The awake, aware and compassionate Provider is driving the team with material support (food, shelter, finances, tools, facilities, connections) and inspiring those around her to push through to completion.

Motivating Providers make fabulous behind the scenes supporters. When you are putting a team together, be sure you have some "Round People" in your group.

In the less aware person, the round shape can come through as someone who is co-dependent or too accommodating. She may fixate on winning approval and love by giving away too much of herself while trying to please others, especially if she has a deep Cupid's Bow. The danger is that this way of connecting can lead to one feeling used or victimized. A round lip print calls the person to embrace her natural people skills and to connect to her abilities in ways that empower her and do not deplete her. We're talking about inner empowerment of course, not power over others.

Actress Angelina Jolie expresses as a Provider, both as a mother who supports her family beautifully, and as a humanitarian who has worked with UNHCR, a United Nations organization that provides food, water, shelter and medical assistance to refugees. This is the perfect expression of a round lip print. Oprah Winfrey expressed the round lip print when she built a school for teen-aged girls in South Africa. In fact, I call the Round lip print the "Oprah" lip print!

Your invitation, if you have a round lip print, is to aim high when setting your goals. You are being called on to set an example of cooperation and to model adaptability.

Center yourself in the power of who you are. Allow yourself to flow into your purpose. Your evolutionary process includes serving the needs of others in any variety of ways. But it's important that your service comes from an empowered perspective and a willing heart, and never from resentment or feeling put upon. Check in with yourself, set boundaries and move forward in the most loving and harmonious way.

More on the Symbolism of "Round"

Print 11: Round Lip Print

The circle is a powerful geometric shape that occurs in almost infinite ways in the world around us. Everywhere you look in nature you'll see things that are round, spherical or tubular, or that move in a circular direction. The Sun, the Moon, and the Stars are circles in the sky with orbits that make even larger circles. Cut into a tomato, an onion, a banana or a tree and you'll find a circle. Pebbles, flowers, planets, snowflakes, eyes and their pupils, Brussels sprouts and water drops are round. Tornados, hurricanes, whirlpools and volcanoes are expressions of round going somewhere fast! Time moves in a circle as the sun rises and sets each day and the hours and seasons do their turn around us year in and year out. Hugs are round.

Speaking to the mystical and spiritual aspects of the circle, Black Elk, a famous Lakota Medicine Man and clairvoyant said:

> *"Everything the Power of the World does is done in a circle. The sky is round and I have heard that the earth is round like a ball, and so are all the stars. The wind, in its greatest power, whirls. Birds make their nests in circles, for theirs is the same religion as ours.*
>
> *The sun comes forth and goes down again in a circle. The moon does the same and both are round. Even the seasons form a great circle in their changing and always come back to where they were. The life of a man is a circle, from childhood to childhood ... and so it is with everything where power moves."*

Your round lip print is one more of the multitude of circles in the natural world. As such, it holds the power of unity, continuity and renewal, cycles of death and rebirth, transformation, protection, infinity, wholeness and connection of all things to all other things in creation. The concept of unity and interrelatedness pervades the round lip print. In addition, you are compelled by nature to keep things moving forward toward

Print 12: Round Lip Print

completion, and as such, you exist in harmony with the resonance and momentum of the Universe as it spins ever outward toward its infinite edges.

If you are "Round," stay present and don't get so caught up in the "doing" and "achieving" that you disconnect from "being." Your Round nature wants to be of service, to create supply where there is demand, to harmonize with balance and fluidity and to move forward productively. Learn to roll with the eternal moment of now with non-resistance to "what is" even as "what is" morphs and flows in a never-ending continuum of change.

SQUARE AND RECTANGLE
The Problem Solver

  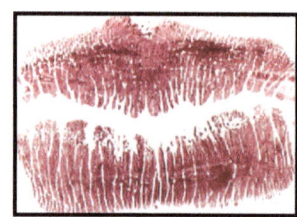

The **SQUARE** and the **RECTANGLE** express the same personality traits. Notice in these examples that some prints classified as this shape are not geometrically pure. Maybe the corners are a bit tapered or there is a rounded quality or a protrusion somewhere. But we are not geometric beings, and our lip prints are not digitally created, so what we are looking for is the strongest suggestion of a shape. If we see more than one shape in the same print, than we are looking at a hybrid lip print that holds the qualities of both shapes.

But back to "Square One." This is the shape of the **Problem Solver**. Jilly Eddy, the mother of Lipsology™, calls this shape the "Godfather/Godmother Lip Print," as this shape indicates someone who can make the problem "go away" like the Godfather portrayed by Marlon Brando, or make your wishes come true, like the Godmother in the story of Cinderella. I am reminded of Harry Truman when I see this shape; a president who personified the responsibility of his office when he said, "The buck stops here." The owners of square lip prints are the Harry Trumans of their home and work environment. The buck stops with them. They are good at solving their own problems and are willing to help others with theirs. They are the personification of the "imperative of responsibility."

Your coworker who says, "Don't worry . . . I'll take care of it," the assistant who finds a hotel and flight for her boss when everything is sold out, the politician who negotiates a peace agreement, the handyman who finds the mysterious leak in the plumbing, the real estate agent who helps negotiate a difficult deal, these are the Problem Solvers among us.

People who express as square lip prints are often the pillars of our society. They are the inventors like Thomas Edison, the political ground breakers like Franklin D. Roosevelt and philanthropists like John D Rockefeller, Jr. Problem Solvers are willing to take on responsibility and see things through until a solution is found. Theirs is the gift of foresight . . . the ability to see through the illusion of the problem to the eventual and inevitable solution. They persevere, forge ahead and in doing so, they often discover new solutions for all of us.

The Importance of Being Square

The energy of the "Square" is a powerful way of being. Problem Solvers are known for being responsible, reliable and solid. They are handy in the area of their expertise and skill sets and are instrumental in making life easier and safer for the rest of us. Somewhere inside of every "Square" person is a strong and dependable warrior-for-good. I'm certain that if we put lipstick on our military soldiers, we'd find that we have an abundance of square lip prints in the ranks of our armed services.

There are two important factors to remember if you have a square lip print. First, Problem Solvers can get snagged by the drama around them and find themselves taking on too many problems to solve because of their desire to conquer the problem at hand. This can result in one feeling overwhelmed. It's easy to cross the line from productivity to a loss of focus that engenders procrastination, and ultimately an inability to solve any problems at all.

Unchecked, the stress of having too much to do can become a pattern that traps one in a self-made box resembling the shape of one's lip print. When this happens, it is wise to recognize one's limitations, to set boundaries, to learn to say "I can't help just now" and when appropriate, to ask for help.

Second, a Problem Solver should consider whether helping someone solve a problem will empower that person or enable that person. What empowers others will empower you. What enables others will disempower you. If your son asks you to help him with his math homework, and you guide him so that he can find the solutions to the problems, that empowers him. You don't help him by doing his homework for him. Set a firm intention: Empower, don't enable. Once again, this is best done by setting clear boundaries.

We observe expressions of the Problem Solver in people like the rock star Bono with "African Debt Relief," Former President Clinton's "Clinton Global Initiative," Former Secretary of State Madeleine Albright, Bill and Melinda Gates, and the late Steve Jobs. Problem Solvers are natural philanthropists, and they find pleasure in volunteering for organizations that are proactively serving communal needs. They are perceived as a steady and solid presence in the lives of those they know and encounter. People depend on them.

Your invitation as a Problem Solver is to willingly and gratefully accept the responsibility of your calling while still honoring your own real-time limits and abilities. Remember that you are important to those who know, love and depend on you. Open your heart and give without judgment or agenda and without marginalizing yourself or enabling the dependency of others. You do not serve the purposes of your calling if you allow yourself to be depleted in the process. Love yourself and appreciate the abilities you are called to share. Walk in power as the strong and dependable Problem Solver that you came here to be. In your hands, problems are simply solutions waiting to happen.

The Symbolism of the Rectangle and the Square

Not surprisingly, the square and rectangle represent the number 4. In numerology, four is the number of stability and foundations. Fours are hard workers and they expect others to work hard as well. They like order and productivity. Four is practical, disciplined, industrious and responsible. Your four-sided lip print speaks to your willingness to be a support structure for those around you, and like that structure, you may be rigid in your beliefs, especially if your "lips are sealed" or positioned very close together in your prints.

In many indigenous American traditions four also represents the four directions (north, south, east, and west), the four worlds (animal, mineral, plants and humans), the four elements (earth, air, fire and water), the four seasons (spring, summer, autumn, winter), and the four aspects of a human (physical, mental, emotional, spiritual).

The Maoris of New Zealand teach that one should seek four perspectives on every situation in order to find the truth.

Owners of the square and rectangular lip print tend to be pragmatic, logical and down to earth. They are grounded in practicality and sometimes literal to the extreme. Four represents power, stability, foundations and support, solidity, home base, security and endurance, the location of the light left on at night for the prodigal son or passing stranger.

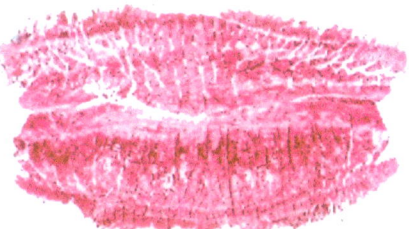

Print 13: Rectangular Lip Print

In Japan the square is a sacred shape, symbolizing opening to the presence of the Divine. Japanese tea houses are square, and are intended to support the participants of a tea ceremony in remaining in the present Divine Moment, and engaging in a ceremony performed with precision and reverence.

If you have a four-sided lip print, you are meant to know and own your strength. You are here to stand tall in your integrity and to shoulder responsibility in the clear understanding that you can weather any difficulty by staying present and quieting the mind and emotions.

If you have a rectangular lip print with the lips close together, you appreciate traditions and rituals, and it is up to you to pass along your knowledge to the next generation. You will navigate toward solutions with conservative caution. Along the way, check in with your closest-held beliefs and be willing to discard any outdated opinions that no longer serve you, or that are no longer the truth.

Print 14: Square Lip Print

If your lip print is open in a square, as in print 14, you are more likely to be open to the gateways of new thought and perspectives, but again only those based on solid practicality and usefulness. In either case, rectangular or square, remember

THE MEANING OF SHAPES | 53

that you are one of the people in your communal arena upon whom others depend for stability and solutions. You're an anchor, the frame around the landscape of life in which the rest of us are experiencing this physical world.

TRIANGLE
The Mentor

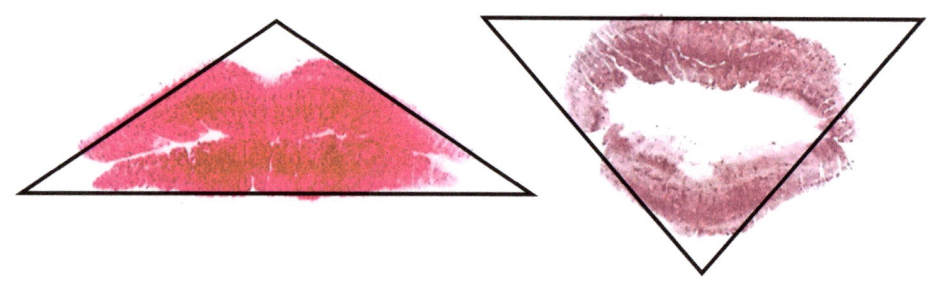

The lip print that has the shape of the **Triangle** is found on people who are **Mentors**. To identify a triangular lip print, look for a flat side on the upper or lower lip, and a pointed side on the other lip.

Your first grade teacher, your parents, your big brother, your basketball coach, your boss, your doctor, your real estate agent, your minister, the woman behind the man, the wind beneath the wings . . . they are the behind the scenes support system that impels us to succeed. Where would any of us be without all of the people who have coached, advised and taught us throughout our life?

People who exemplify the dynamic of the Mentor are the late Nelson Mandela, Dr. Phil, Doreen Virtue, Music Producer David Foster, Dr. John Demartini and Marianne Williamson.

It's not unusual to see a hybrid of the round and the triangle, in which case you have someone who mentors and offers material support.

Importance of Being Triangular

From the time we are born we are surrounded by people teaching us how to walk, talk, read, write, do math, tie our shoes, use a computer, drive, cook, dress, and balance our bank statements. Life is an ongoing process of learning and there is no shortage of people who can and do contribute to our base of knowledge as we grow up. But not everyone who draws a paycheck as a teacher, instructor or guide is a true Mentor. A true Mentor recognizes and believes in the talents and abilities of his protégés and does not buy into their self-imposed limitations. He supports their shining by offering wisdom, teachings and guidance in creative and practical ways. He knows how to communicate with clarity and compassion. He holds a big vision for his mentees, and suffers no excuses.

True Mentors uplift us and find joy and purpose in seeing us succeed. They are consciously committed to the service of teaching and supporting the development of autonomous human beings. Their mission is to discover the hidden gemstone in others. A Mentor helps others move through their self-defeating illusions of failure into the light of their own abilities.

The Mentor differs, then, from the Round Provider in that the first supports the success of others emotionally, spiritually and intellectually and the second gives material and tangible support.

Your invitation as the Mentor is to teach with conscious intention, and from your heart. Kindness, compassion, generosity and true affection for your protégés will do as much to encourage them as the wisest advice you could give. But strive to be wise, as well. Step out of complacency and give attention to your own mental, emotional, and spiritual education. Ask frequently for Grace to guide your thoughts and words in every interaction, so that your presence as a Mentor may be of benefit and blessing to others.

The Symbolism of the Triangular

In Homer's epic poem, *The Odyssey*, Mentor was a friend of Odysseus (aka Ulysses). When Odysseus leaves home to fight in the Trojan Wars, he asks Mentor to look after his palace and his son in his absence. Mentor raises the child of his friend for ten years until Odysseus returns.

This is where the term "Mentor" comes from. The word implies a parental relationship between a teacher and a student. It further suggests a certain amount of affection and a deeper connection than what we might imagine coming from an "instructor." The true

Mentor is 100% committed to the success of those he guides and will always and naturally find his own success through this channel of self-expression and generosity.

With this in mind, let's address the difference between the triangle seated on its base (the upright triangle) and the inverted triangle. When we look at an upright triangle, we see something solid and stable, reminiscent of the eternal-seeming Egyptian and Aztec pyramids. There is a powerful, masculine energy to such a structure, well-grounded and planted in place.

Print 15: Triangle (Upright) Lip Print

Historians have suggested that the shape of the pyramids built in ancient civilizations was intended to direct the mind upward, to inspire mental and spiritual ascension. The soaring lines of a pyramid invite the onlooker's gaze to move toward the heavens. Who could stand at the base of The Pyramids of Giza, just outside of Cairo, without feeling pulled up to a higher perspective?

Just like the rock-solid pyramid, the true Mentor steadily supports the ascension of others. You are strong and stable enough to carry the weight of the aspirations of those you teach, coach, encourage and inspire. Once again, this does not preclude your own ascension and success. You are often a gifted leader; otherwise people would not be inclined to listen to you. You may be the "structure" that supports others in their climb to the top, but they are only climbing to where you already stand, metaphorically.

Print 16: Triangle (Inverted) Lip Print

Your strength is in knowing what works and sticking to it. Once you have discovered your most successful form of expression as a Mentor, you find innovative ways to honor what has worked before. You create mentoring rituals for your protégés. You are the basketball coach who puts your team through daily drills over and over until they are making those three pointers consistently. You help your protégés build a foundation of skills and self-esteem that will support a lifetime of success. Remember to maintain your heart connection . . . your true Mentor connection.

Conversely, when we look at the inverted triangle (a triangle balanced on its tip-toes), we are not seeing a fixed and stable structure, but rather one that could tip or lean one way or the other with the possibility that things could change any minute. There is a more receptive, feminine energy to this form of the triangle, an open, anything-can-happen dynamic, and one that is balanced by an inner need to excel.

If your lip print is sitting on a pointed lower lip, you will be a versatile and creative Mentor, always finding new ways to express yourself with those you guide and inspire. You're the interpretive dance teacher, the kindergarten teacher up to your neck in finger paint, the culinary wizard who teaches his students to combine ingredients in exciting and surprising new ways. You're the Mom who teaches her daughter to design and sew her clothes, and the wife who teaches her workaholic husband to maintain an innovative and healthy diet in spite of his schedule. Perhaps you're a yoga teacher like my niece, pictured here. You may be drawn to an "alternative" career path or ideology, or one that allows you to express yourself with freedom and independence.

Your strength is in your proactive creativity. Your guidance is to "stay on your toes," centered and balanced like a beautifully turning top.

In numerology, the triangle's three sides represent the power of the number 3. The qualities of "three" include self-expression and artful communication, which are of great value to you as a Mentor. Phoenix-based Numerologist Rommy Banaszczyk says that the vibration of 3 brings happiness, hope, and joy, and that people with a 3 vibration must share their optimistic point of view with others.

The triangle and the number three can be seen to be consistently carrying the energy of mentoring, communication, teaching, inspiration, and supporting the aspirations of those you are asked to serve. As a Mentor, you achieve your own ambitions by generously helping others to achieve theirs. When you accept the mantle of your Mentor nature, you step into a noble tradition of service that frees you in ways you cannot now imagine as you discover the best in yourself.

DIAMOND
Role Model/Leader

Diamond lip prints will angle to a point on the top and the bottom lips. They do not have to be perfectly centered points.

No one shape is better than any other, but I still hear people say, "I want to be a Diamond Girl!"

Let's face it; diamonds are flashy, brilliant and valuable, and Diamond People are creative, fun and charismatic. They are naturally status conscious, competitive and ambitious. They are usually successful, highly competent and often find themselves, without effort, cast into leadership positions. They are the **Role Model/Leaders**. Whereas the triangle is the shape of the Mentor, the diamond is made up of two triangles, so we have mentor-ship times two. The Role Model/Leader says, "Here's how to succeed . . . watch me and I'll show you what it looks like!"

This is not to say that only Diamonds succeed. Bill Gates and Warren Buffet are most likely Problem Solvers. And don't forget that success can be defined in many ways. A mother who devotes her time to raising balanced, successful children can feel just as much pleasure in her accomplishments as a CEO, rock star or university president. I'm just saying, if you are a Diamond Girl or Guy, there will be accomplishments and there will be a call to mentorship!

The Importance of Being a Diamond

Much of what we learn is through imitation. Those we admire model a way of being and teach us what is possible. A true Diamond is conscious of the power she has to influence those around her. Her intelligence and charisma are used for good and in service to others. This is integral to the authentic success of a Diamond Person, and true Diamonds will not feel satisfied in their success if they do not help and teach others along the way.

As my role model and mentor, KC Miller says, "People will be attracted to you because they think they are like you, or because they want to be like you." If you are a Diamond, you are being called to step onto center stage and let your light shine as you share your blessings and wisdom in ways that teach others how to succeed as you have.

Diamonds are easy to find in the worlds of entertainment, sports, business and politics. Katy Perry, Jennifer Lawrence and Taylor Swift, are likely Diamond Girls. Mohammed Ali, George Clooney, Clint Eastwood, and Barack Obama have all demonstrated the attributes of the diamond shaped lip print.

In the spiritually unconscious person, the power to succeed and influence others can be used in ways that do not ultimately serve anyone but that particular person. Think of any of a number of "Hollywood bad boys" (or girls) who have enjoyed the benefits of their diamond shape without understanding and living up to the responsibilities of being a role model for others. Historical records are rife with political and corporate leaders who rose to power based on their charisma, skills and leadership, but who then turned away from the privilege of mentoring and wise leadership to indulge themselves in the goodies that come with being in charge.

Insecurity or a lack of true self-love will undermine the full expression of this shape and its manifestations. Your Invitation as a Diamond Person is to SHINE! Own your Diamond-essence and step into leadership and mentor-ship with commitment and enthusiasm. You are meant to lead the way, so step forward with care, ever mindful of the fact that others look up to you and will follow your example. Seek to live a life that is worthy of your purpose.

The Symbolism of the Diamond

The Five energy of numerology permeates the diamond-shaped lip print. The diamond is made up of two triangles—one upright triangle on top of one inverted triangle, making a 4-sided diamond bisected by one line, illustrated here.(See following illustration)

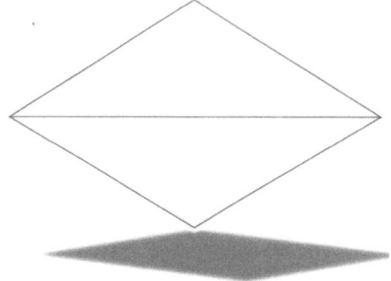

Bisected, 4-sided Diamond

Five and the diamond hold the energy of the innovator and explorer. Five loves change, variety and opportunities. Self-promotion, skillful social interaction, and a creative imagination contribute to the success of the vivacious Five. Five is also the number associated with the planet Mars, with the influences of passion and hyperactivity.

Diamonds, as gemstones, are the most celebrated jewels in the world. They symbolize all of the worldly manifestations of success—fortune, power, luxury, leadership, opportunity, security, abundance and the choices and freedoms that come with wealth. On a spiritual level, diamonds represent inner wealth, healing, purity, clarity, wisdom and transcendence.

Now let's return to the illustration. We see an upright triangle sitting atop an inverted triangle. One reflects the other in a mirror image. What a great metaphor for the role of the Diamond Person—that of modeling success for others and, as Mentors, mirroring back to others what they are doing successfully.

The Diamond is a beautiful combination of masculine power blended with feminine nurturing and receptivity; a blend that results in the chaos of creativity. I have met Diamonds who were inventors, authors, business owners, community leaders, celebrities and successful people of all persuasions and life-paths. There is an upbeat, often joyful exuberance in those Diamonds who are in touch with their natural way of being.

But just as often I read the prints of Diamonds who are not yet aware of their nature and potential, who are still struggling with self-doubt, procrastination, and other forms of self-sabotage. If this is you, it means you just haven't accepted the truth about who you are. Yes, it's that simple. This book will offer you some alternative perspectives to assist you as you move into owning your Diamond-hood!

IRREGULAR
Artsy or Fartsy

Print 17: Irregular Lip Print

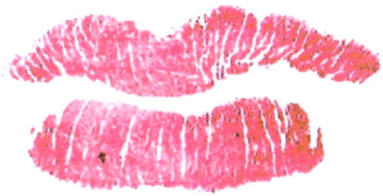

Print 18: Curvy Irregular Lip Print

Print 19: Angular Irregular Lip Print

Every now and then you'll see a lip print that is difficult to define geometrically. Although few lip prints are perfectly symmetrical or perfect squares, triangles, diamonds, etc., an irregular lip print will have, bumps, jagged edges and other irregularities that pull on or distort the geometric shape enough to influence the general outline. You may be able to see a suggestion of one of the geometric shapes we have discussed previously, in which case, you could apply those traits in the reading. But you'll also see angles, extensions and protrusions, or there may be lots of curviness, with undulations and movement in the outline of the lips. The **Curvy Irregular** and the **Angular Irregular** each demand to be in a class of their own.

An irregular lip print may represent three distinctive aspects of a person. The owner of the lips may be a combination of two or more of those aspects, or distinctively one of the three.

The first, the **Curvy Irregular** is the one I call **"Artsy."** Here we find the creative/artistic aspect of a person. Fun, imaginative, inspirational to others, gifted, talented, joyful, funny, this irregular is the shining star of irregularity! She may be an artist or performer or just a very active and happy person with a ready laugh.

You may see this curvy outline on one or both of the lips. The upper lip represents how we present ourselves out in the world, so curviness here would say that the person is very creative in ways that others notice. When the curviness is on the lower lip, it represents a kind of creativity that others may not see on display. Either the person is

THE MEANING OF SHAPES | 61

a closet artist, or writer, or inventor, or gourmet chef for example, or she is not using or even acknowledging her creative talents.

Print 20: "Artsy"

Print 21: "Fartsy"

When the curvy lines are on both lips, you have someone who is expressing her inner talents in a public way. Print 20 is a print made by a professional artist. She creates elegant oil paintings that she sells at her own art gallery in Scottsdale, Arizona. She is also a Shaman and an intuitive healer.

The second possible interpretation of the Irregular lip print is the **"Fartsy,"** or the moody curmudgeon aspect. These prints are often more **Angular Irregulars**. See prints 19 and 21. They can still be very creative, but like the grumpy old man who lives next door, this person is unpredictable and you never know what kind of a mood he'll be in the next time you see him. He may be warm and jovial, or as prickly as a porcupine. He is as changeable as the weather. He can be an over-thinker, analytical, shrewd, and highly sensitive. Inconsistency, a need for drama, and an uneven temper are typical in this lip print type. You might feel a need to be cautious when in his presence. He may live in an "all glasses are half-empty" and "get off my lawn" kind of world.

Take a look at these examples of a "joyful" Irregular. (Prints 22 and 23) Both prints are from the same person. I read this man's lip prints at a corporate event. It was evident

Print 22: Irregular Lip Print

Print 23: Irregular Lip Print

that he was well-loved by his co-workers, and by the time I was finished with his reading, I loved him too! He was expansively fun and warm with a creative and spontaneous sense of humor. There are lots of curvy places on both the upper and lower lips. We also see some more angular protrusions, indicating a shaper side to his personality, which was not in evidence when I met him. He is definitely an Artsy/Fartsy combination! We spent about 10 minutes talking, surrounded by a crowd of people who seemed to hold him in high regard. He is not someone I will soon forget. I can't look at these prints without smiling.

Print 24: Curvy/Angular Irregular   **Print 25:** Curvy/Angular Irregular

Prints 24 and 25 are two more examples of the combination of the Curvy and the Angular. As you would expect, these can be read as creative folks who are funny, charismatic, challenging, sensitive, idiosyncratic, or pushy but never, ever boring.

Print 26: Curvy Irregular Square

Let's look at how a secondary shape can temper the meaning of irregularities in a lip print. This print is actually a hybrid of the Square and the Curvy Irregular. It belongs to a cello player who performs in an all-female electric string quartet. The band performs original and top of the chart rock music and they are building an international name for themselves. She has a very clear squareness to her print, plus the curves that suggest originality. She is indeed the down-to-earth, dependable Problem Solver that this shape suggests. She is mature and a patient mother to her three year-old girl, and when she's on stage, her curvy creativity and exuberance emerges and she rocks the house!

THE MEANING OF SHAPES | 63

The third type of irregular lip print is the **Traumatic Irregular**. There has been some kind of **trauma** experienced by the person. It can be mental, emotional or physical disturbance. It may be a temporary or chronic condition. But it is a situation that has changed the energetic field of the person involved in some traumatic way. So this is not "Artsy" or "Fartsy," but an indication that there is upset and that something has gone awry for the person whose lip prints these are. Compassion is in order.

Print 27: Kiss Card Displaying Emotional Trauma

Irregular lip prints that show **emotional trauma**, upheaval or upset can show up in the midst of an otherwise standard set of lip prints from the same person. For example, print 27 is a Kiss Card made by someone who had recently separated from her husband.

At the time that she made this Kiss Card, she was in the process of relocating to a new city with no job in place, leaving behind all that was familiar and comfortable, including several pets.

The lip print on the far right is in the position of her present thoughts about the future. On her card you can see her discomfort when she thinks ahead, as the lip print is twisted off of its center and has begun to take on the look of something from a Salvador Dali painting.

Her first two prints are beautiful hybrids of the Mentor (Triangle) and the Problem Solver (Square), but the third print begins to collapse on itself, giving way at the corners and tilting into a kind of parallelogram. She is feeling off-center, ungrounded, fearful of the future, but believes that she must urgently push forward, (evidenced by the bump on the top of her lip) even as she is resisting these changes in her life. No wonder, with all of the push and pull, that we see the "structure" of her future life appearing to collapse. Let me point out that the "collapse" is within her imagination when she thinks about the future and is not a prediction. Two years later, she is, in fact, in a new and loving relationship and appears to be very happy.

When I took the print in print 28, the owner of the print was getting a divorce from an unfaithful husband and trying to save her home from foreclosure. Imagine how that could

Print 28: Traumatic Irregular

Print 29: Traumatic Irregular

unseat your balance and then look at her lip print. Notice how similar it is to the third print on the previous card.

For a while, I came to think of this type of print as the "divorce lip print," but I have also seen it in situations where someone is fearful of losing her job, her home, or of facing something new and unknown.

The lower lip holds information about our self-perception and security, and when that gets skewed, so does our lower lip. If there is irregularity, there may be some kind of inner turmoil that is pulling the print out of symmetry, as if a rug has been pulled out from beneath the person.

An Irregular lip print may be caused by a temporary anomaly that will pass in time. It may also be the product of an injury or a **physical disability**, as is the print in print 29. The print is Irregular in that the upper lip is missing. When you see part of the lip print missing, you are usually, though not always, looking at some kind of physical trauma. We'll discuss this in full when we get to "Missing Parts."

The Importance of Being Irregular

The Irregular lip print is powerful in its singularity and carries a loaded message to its owner. That message could be one of validation for the creative life force energy the person is harboring . . . or one of caution; signaling that there is a need for maturation or that help or counseling may be a prudent course of action.

There are many situations that can cause a lip print to migrate from a regular geometric shape into an irregular one. An Irregular lip print can seem chaotic in form, but remember that out of chaos comes original thought and eventually, order. Consider each print with an open and non-judgmental heart and with the utmost kindness and understanding. Every lip print holds a message of guidance and insight for its owner. Use your knowledge and intuition to articulate what the lips want to say.

If you find yourself looking at an Irregular lip print in a reading for someone, gently explore the following possibilities. Is the subject artistic, quirky, and unique? Is he bubbling with enthusiasm for life, or does he seem moody, grumpy, and thin-skinned? Could some trauma be going on?

A few well-directed questions will give clues as to how to interpret this shape. You may be looking at a gifted artistic genius, or someone experiencing a difficult time, or the crabby complainer that others avoid. Remember, even the prickliest curmudgeon contributes to our human story. Respect his space and affirm his creativity and gifts, and move on to the other indicators in his prints. There is always a message of validation waiting to be shared.

The Symbolism of the Irregular

Irregular lip prints are by definition, unpredictable and chaotic. But, as the Greek Poet Hesiod believed, it is out of the formlessness of chaos that a new order emerges. If you have an irregular lip print, seek ways to mine your imagination, your discomfort, your moodiness, or your trauma for the gold and the gifts hidden within yourself and your experience. There is a new state of being emerging in every moment as the wheel of creation spins potential into reality.

At its best, the Irregular shape represents original thought and expression combined with a unique and luminous viewpoint. With some Irregulars, we see great humor, unbridled passion and a loving heart bursting into our presence like a brilliant sunrise. At its worst an Irregular lip print represents a narrowing of perspective, a restriction of the heart, a fearful or wary stance. Either way, we are being asked in every moment to say "yes" to life and to ourselves, to our gifts and to our experience of the present.

Just say "yes."

HYBRID

Looking at the five shapes, we've seen several examples of lip prints that are a combination of two or more shapes. Hybrid lip prints are not actually a shape, any more than a mutt is a breed of dog. But rather, just as a mixed breed dog will carry the traits of his ancestry, Hybrid prints hold within them the qualities of all of the shapes that they suggest.

People with Hybrid prints are flexible in ways that allow them to intuitively and authentically show up as needed in any situation. There will be the kind of fluidity of expression that we'd expect in a multilingual person at an international cocktail party!

Print 30: Hybrid Lip Print

A real-time example of the Hybrid is the owner of this Print 30. He is an 18-year-old who volunteered in 2014 to spend his spring break building a school in Ghana, Africa, with a corps of other volunteers. His print is a combination of the Diamond, the Round, and the Square. It holds the qualities of the Role Model/Leader, the Motivating Provider, and the Problem Solver.

Shapes Shape Your Life

Finally . . .

It's possible that until now you haven't paid close attention to how you tend to "be" with others, so begin noticing now. Notice when you feel you have successfully interacted with others and when you haven't. Check in with what you know about your shape. Were you standing in the authenticity of your natural "Path of Purpose" when things worked for you? And where were you standing when they didn't? Don't judge yourself when things don't go well. Just notice and then strive to be intentional about your natural strengths in each moment.

Take a few minutes to consider which shapes and which pathway of service each person might be expressing.

CLARITY

Before we move on, there is one more observation I have made about the outer edge of a lip print. Some lip prints will have clearly defined edges, so precise that they look as though they were cut with a razor. Others will have less defined borders and they may even look a little messy.

Print 31: Clarity Lip Print

The clearer the outline, the more focused, articulate, competitive, literal, and responsible the person is likely to be. These are rule followers who prefer to color within the lines that they themselves have drawn. They will operate within the boundaries that they have constructed, and they will do so with precision. They may be prone to stress.

When the outer edge of the lip print is interrupted by "solar flares" of energy, when it becomes less precise and blurrier, we have more of a sprawling thought process, or possibly someone who doesn't know how to set clear boundaries for himself. There may be unchecked patterns of behavior or temperament that interfere with social relationships. There could be a tendency towards self-indulgence or feelings of victim-hood. And, as in the Irregular print, there may be a wildly creative imagination, flamboyance and gusto for life, with few confining boundaries.

Print 32: Kiss Card Displaying Smudged Edges

FULLNESS

In our current culture, full lips are considered voluptuous, sensuous, and sexy. Some women have Gortex® implants surgically inserted into their lips, or they have "dermal material" injected to make the lips appear younger and fuller. Others just paint outside the lines with their lipstick . . . with varying results.

It is true that our lips become thinner as we age, so fuller lips suggest youth. Studies have shown that the more estrogen in a woman's body, the fuller her lips are and the more fertile she is. Genetic programming in the male human automatically telegraphs the message that someone with fuller lips is the best one with whom to mate. But even young women can have thin lips . . . so what does that "say" about them?

If we look at Hollywood typecasting, we think of such classic characters as Frau Blucher in *Young Frankenstein*. Portrayed by Cloris Leachman, an actress who actually has a very voluptuous lower lip, she was made up to appear to have thin lips and was, as a character, cold, calculating, dry, suspicious, and sexually repressed.

But is that fair? Are thin-lipped people more sexually repressed or less attractive than those with fuller lips? Are they cold and calculating, as the Wicked Witch of the West was in the *Wizard of Oz*? Of course not!

In Defense of Thin Lips

Thin lips may appear in pairs, or as singles coupled with a fuller lip. One may have a thin upper lip and a thin lower lip, a full upper and a thin lower, or a thin upper and a full lower lip.

The first thing to know is that the upper lip is your "listening, learning, thinking and gathering" lip, and the lower lip is your "teaching, speaking, singing, writing and dispersing" lip. The fullness of the upper lip represents the width or scope of your interests and gathering of information, and how attentive you will be to any particular conversation. It will be some indication of how focused your mind is when you are working or speaking to others. The fullness of the lower lip will indicate your willingness to participate in conversations that do or do not involve your areas of interest, and how articulate you are on specific or general topics. It will indicate your style of "dispersing" what you know.

Print 33: Thin Upper Lip Print

A thin upper lip (Print 33) does not mean that you are not a good listener, although you may be perceived that way. It means that you are a specialist. You're a focused and particular listener and learner. The subjects and concepts that are useful and interesting to you will get your full concentration, and those that aren't, won't. You will be interested in learning about a specific field of interest.

So when the upper lip is thin, we have a person who focuses on whatever she is doing in the moment and who generally has little time for or interest in small talk. If you walk into her office while she is working, don't expect her to stop everything and listen to the details of your latest argument with your boyfriend. You're better off finding someone down the hall with a fuller upper lip who will be delighted to hear every detail! But if you interrupt her with a question or information about what she is working on, you will have her undivided attention.

Our thin upper-lipped person may find it excruciating to attend a cocktail party unless it is peopled with others who share her interests. Watch her eyes glass over while the local gossip monger opines on who's doing what with whom. She is soooo not interested!

As you might expect, thin lips come with a certain amount of perfectionism and sensitivity. These folks can be highly principled, with a strong sense of ethics. They may be impatient with themselves and others. Narrow lipped people are organized and fastidious and can drive themselves and others crazy striving for the perfect outcome.

If you belong to this "club" your curriculum in life includes finding the balance between your desire for perfection in yourself and others and making peace with the results of everyone's best efforts. Learn to soften to yourself and your expectations. Allow excellence to be good enough. Notice when you are obsessing and being overly critical. Make a choice to relax and allow yourself to be human, to make mistakes and to do things imperfectly.

Print 34: Thin Lower Lip Print

If you have a thin lower lip, (Print 34) your friends and family might say that it's like pulling teeth to get you to talk sometimes. You prefer to talk about, write about, and/or teach about your passions and interests. You can sit all evening at a dinner party without uttering a word until someone asks you about your work, or your family, or your hobbies, or anything that excites you, and then, "Whoa! Nelly!" You'll join into the conversation with gusto! Again, a thin lower lip does not mean that you are quiet or uncommunicative. It does mean that you won't waste breath and words on what you consider trivial. You have a gift for the specific. If you have a thin lower lip you can be frugal or prudent with your money. You might make a great mathematician, accountant, scientist, engineer, surgeon or musician.

Your focus can be intense on anything that interests you. You deal in details and dissecting the elements of the whole; putting them back together . . . perfectly. As teachers, those with thin lower lips will hold their students to the very high standard that they have set for themselves. The sophisticated artistry of the works of Japanese architect Kenzo Tange, the writings of biologist and environmentalist Rachel Carson, the intricate renderings of birds illustrated by John James Audubon, are all examples of what you can expect from a thin lower-lipped person.

Print 35: Thin Thin Lip Print

If someone has both a thin upper and lower lip, (Print 35) then you can expect laser-like attention to organization and specific interests. This is a person who finds it hard to delegate, as no one will do it as well as she will! This particular print belongs to a woman who teaches a very specialized kind of spiritual training. She has built a business around her specialty and has published a book on the subject. Her communication skills are prolific when she is talking or writing about what she teaches, and yet in social situations she can sometimes be the quiet one at the table.

Twin thin lips require a high vibrational conversation, and can't be bothered wasting their listening or words on trivialities.

Combinations

Print 36: Full Upper Lip Print

Print 37: Full Lower Lip Print

Print 38: Varied Fullness

When the upper lip is full and the lower lip is thin, as in Print 36, we are still looking at the lip print of a specialist. The broader upper lip shows a widely explored scope of learning in a specialized field, to the point of expertise. This print on the left belongs to an engineer who has an impressive education and who travels world-wide as an executive of an international corporation. He has mastered his field of work. When it comes to "listening and learning," the emphasis here is on the "learning" regarding his career, and "listening" to all that pertains to it. His children will complain with good humor that he zones out on them. His thoughts are often on his business, for which he has a passion. But his full upper lip suggests that he is much more aware and attentive than his children think. He may prefer to talk about his work, or not speak at all, but when he turns his attention toward you, he is a generous listener. Someone with lips like these will keep your secrets, simply because he's not interested in talking about your story.

The owner of a full lower lip and a thin upper lip is a charming, articulate conversationalist and teacher. (Print 37) With the focus of her upper lip and the fluidity of her speaking skills, prepare to be swept away if her attention is on you! She can be the most charming and persuasive of our thin-full combinations. However, you may be left with the impression that she would rather talk than listen, and you'd be right, unless you are talking to her interests.

Sometimes the fullness of the lips is mixed horizontally as in Print 38. One side or another of the upper or lower lip is full and one side is thin. In a print like this we see someone who may swing from inward focused attention to open and easy communication in social situations. Because there

Print 39: Combo Fullness Lip Print

is some irregularity, we would do well to make no assumptions as to which aspect we'll encounter on any given day!

We often see an upper lip where the center of the upper lip, known as the Hug Pucker, is full and the right and left sides are thin. (Print 39) This is a person who is an attentive and specialized learner and thinker, but who always has a ready ear for those who are dear to her heart. She will be focused and hands-on at work, but at the end of the day she's all ears when her children climb up into her lap. If you are special to her, she has the time and patience to listen to whatever you have to say.

Once again, a variable fullness combines the attributes of both the thin and full lip, and will indicate an ebb and flow between the two extremes.

And what about the repressed sexuality implied in our culture? Just not true. A thin-lipped lover is just as passionate as a full-lipped lover, and once you have his attention, he will try to be the perfect lover! Encourage him to make do with being excellent . . . .

The Full Skinny on Full Lips!

Print 40: Full Lips

Print 41: Full Upper Lip

If having thin lips is like performing on the balance beam in gymnastics, having full lips is like performing in the floor exercise. There's a broader area in which to play. Another analogy might be a broadband transmission signal over which a wide range of frequencies travel from one technological device to another. The broader your upper lip, the more "stations" your ears and mind will receive.

Again, think of the width and fullness of your lip as an indicator of the spectrum, broad or narrow, of subjects that you are interested in listening to (upper) and talking about (lower). Full-lipped people (Prints 40 and 41) are generous with their knowledge and with their money when they have it; and with yours when they don't. They can create and manage a big vision in life, and they are good at delegating; an important talent when one undertakes complex goals.

FULLNESS | 75

A full upper lip is the sign of someone who has her "listening ears" on most of the time. She is available for listening to a wide range of ideas and content. This does not imply that she will "listen" to you in the sense that she will take your advice or direction.

That will depend on other indicators, like the presence or absence of a Cupid's Bow. But she has "generous ears" and will be genuinely more engaged with you when you "just want to talk" than a thinner lipped person may be, especially if both lips are full.

Again, an exception to this may occur when the lower lip is thin. You may be talking to an engineer, numbers or science person who will only be all ears if you are talking about the subjects he loves.

Print 42: Full Lower Lip Print

Print 43: Equal Fullness

The full lower lip (Print 42) indicates someone with communication skills. By "skills" we mean someone who can talk about almost anything, participate in nearly any conversation, and who never met a stranger, human or animal, especially when the upper lip is full as well. In this case we actually do have someone with a gift for communicating, because listening is at least as important as speaking!

This brings us to another point: When the upper and lower lips are the same fullness, shown here in Print 43, whether thin or full or somewhere in between, it indicates a gift for teaching. When the listening matches the speaking, we have someone who takes in either very specialized information (thin lips) or a broad array of informational components (full lips) and reproduces it all through some form of outward communication. Whether it is writing, speaking, mathematics, singing or some other modality it will be done in a way that is faithful to the original content and concepts.

Various examples of fullness:

Print 44: Anthony's Lip Print

Anthony Mazzella

Print 44 is the lip print of a musician named Anthony Mazzella. He writes and plays complex musical arrangements for the guitar. His intricate work is filled with notes that take you by the ears and lead you out of your body and off the planet into space in a rush of euphoric auditory ecstasy. He doesn't sing. He communicates through musical mathematics executed with perfection and artistry, and so we would expect him to have a thin upper and lower lip. That bump of fullness on the lower lip suggests not only his creativity, but that he can turn his analytical, mathematical interpretations outward in a way that reaches others with a resonant and abundant richness. (Find his music at www.anthonymazzella.com.)

Compare his varied fullness to another print with a different kind of varied fullness.

Print 45 belongs to a jazz singer who plays piano and sings very intricate lyrics. She is someone who mesmerizes the audience with her soulful and sexy tonality and whose sensual song choices leave one yearning for candlelight and a warm dance partner. Her lip print is small, giving her control over the detailed lyrics, but full, giving her well-rounded "vocal delivery" abilities. We see the focus and perfectionism needed to sing lyrically complex songs, as the upper and lower lips run to the right becoming thinner and more specialized.

Print 45: Varied Fullness

FULLNESS | 77

Print 46: Singer/Writer

Print 47: Comedian

Print 46 is another singer/songwriter who focuses on captivating and transformative listening experience. With the fullness of her auditory talent she captures the nuances of tone, melodies and lyrics. Her expansive lower lip indicates her gift for interpreting those nuanced components and delivering a performance that connects us to the singer and to the song.

Sometimes the full lower lip demonstrates comedic or acting abilities, or skills in news commentating. Print 47 belongs to a professional comedian. If you start looking, you'll begin to notice how many people you see on TV or in public venues have a full lower lip. These people are the most comfortable, as a group, with public speaking, performing, or leading. Watch the news and look at lower lips. When you're at the movies, check out the fullness of the lower lips on the actors. It's no surprise that we are attracted to people with full lips . . . it seems so many of them are successful or in positions of leadership. Somehow subliminally, if we are of a certain generation or younger, our exposure to 24 hour a day media has caused us to conflate full lips with having money and romance.

In reality there are many examples of thin-lipped people who have achieved success and positions of leadership, and who have led passionate, creative and satisfying lives. They just may not generally be as publicly vocal as their full-lipped brothers and sisters.

Here's a fun thing to play with: If you were to choose one of the following professionals to work with, which ones would you want to have a full upper lip, and which might serve you better with a thin upper lip? Which ones would you prefer to have a full lower lip, based on what you now know about fullness? Would you be better off if any of these had a thin lower lip?

A family doctor

An oncologist

A marriage counselor

A political representative

A realtor

A lawyer

An interior designer

An architect

Which ones would you hope would have the capacity to listen to your needs and concerns? Would it be a strength to have one of these be a little less available to your opinion and a little more focused on doing the job the way he knows it should be done? Would you be expecting ongoing communication from any of these, or would it be OK if your communications were limited to certain schedules and locations? There's one caveat I want to remind you of: you cannot know exactly how full the lips are until you see the print.

The lips on the left made Print 48.

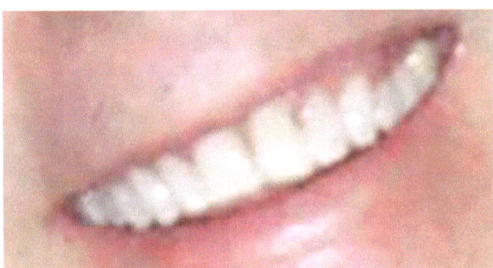 

Print 48: Thin Lips

You always go by the print. Without the print, most everything you assume from looking at someone's mouth is conjecture . . . and that applies to the guesswork, albeit educated guesswork, concerning the celebrities I have mentioned in this book.

The Middle Road

What about somewhere in the middle? That is, the middle point of fullness that the rest of us fall into? Medium fullness represents the average; an average amount of attention will be paid to you by the average fullness listener. Attention may wander at times, and at other times your average listener will be present to what you want to talk about. If her lower lip is of average fullness, she will participate in the conversation, but will not usually dominate it.

And then there is this quote I recently came across:

"I just realized my lips are inside out. They should be turned inwards, because I spend most of my time talking to myself." Jarod Kintz – Nomadic Philosopher

This got me thinking . . . could this be a valid observation about people with thin lips who are perceived as quiet or tuned out? Are they really just too busy to talk, listen or focus on you because they are fully engaged in a conversation with themselves? Hmmmm…

Relatively Speaking

It is useful to look at the relative fullness between the upper and lower lip. A thin upper lip that is thinner than a thin lower lip will hold a similar dynamic as the thin upper and the medium or full lower, for example.

It's best to read the meaning of each lip and then look at how they relate to each other.

POSITION
TIC-TAC-TOE

The position of prints on the paper has significance in Lip Print Reading. When you look at positions of the prints, imagine the Kiss Card is divided into 9 zones, like a Tic-Tac-Toe board, each having to do with time and state of mind.

Horizontally across the card, we have three "time zones." From left to right, prints made on the left side of the page relate to thoughts and feelings about the past. It could be something that happened yesterday, decades ago, or five minutes ago. Prints made in the center relate to thoughts and feelings about the present and prints on the right relate to thoughts and feelings about the future. All of the thinking and feeling is happening *in the present* at the moment the prints are made. In the positioning we can observe how the subject is processing emotions, thoughts, and feelings in the present about the past, present and future.

From the top to the bottom, we see that the top third of the page indicates a sense of dreaming, reminiscing, planning, hoping or envisioning, or you could say our mental and spiritual preoccupations. People whose prints are primarily in this zone may find it difficult to take the action needed to manifest their dreams and plans. They may benefit by finding ways to "ground" themselves. The middle third again brings us back into a more physical and practical presence, or who and how we are being in the present regarding the past, present and future. The bottom third concerns our sense of physical and material comfort, safety and security, as well as our possessions.

For example, if the subject's first lip print is centered in the bottom of the page, she is having a real-time experience that concerns her comfort or security. If there is a print on the bottom right, the concerns are more about what might happen, rather than what present reality is. She may be expecting something good, like a raise, and her attention would be on increased comfort and security. That print would be energized rather than depleted. A faded print on the bottom left could suggest that there has been a difficult time of financial loss or some kind of material lack in the past, or if it is dark in color, she might be focused on a time of great material pleasure and abundance.

The intensity of color and order in which the prints are made speaks to how focused the person is on each "time zone" and state of mind.

Read each block of the diagram on the next page and connect to the energy of each position. Remember that Lip Print Reading is not fortune telling. The prints relay messages not about what may happen or what did happen, but about what you are feeling and thinking about the "may" and the "did." They demonstrate what your opinions and feelings are about the past, present and future in the moment you made each print.

CHARTING THE POSITION OF A PRINT

See Each Kiss Card As a Grid

Top Third = Mental - Spiritual, Reminiscing, Planning or Dreaming
Middle Third = Practical – Present Moment, Perspectives, Action
Bottom Third = Physical – Security, Comfort, Appetite
Left Third = View of the **Past**
Middle Third = Experiences of the **Present**
Right Third = Expectations of the **Future**

Kiss Card		
Past Dreaming of how it was or might have been or should have gone (past dreams or plans)	**Present** Thinking of present moment plans and hopes	**Future** Envisioning the future you want or fear
Past Present to how things were, attached to the past	**Present** Here and Now Available to opportunities or just moving through the day	**Future** How you feel about what needs to happen or be done
Past What you have acquired/lost materially in the past	**Present** What you have now (security and comfort or discomfort)	**Future** What you want to have/get or fear losing materially

SPACING

The open area between the lips is called the **Spacing**. Spacing can vary widely on the same person's lip prints and certainly from one person to the next.

Spacing indicates how open-minded someone is. A wide open space between the lips tells the story of an open-minded person willing to hear about and to consider new ideas and adventures, whereas the more closed the space becomes, the more cautious the person.

Print 49: Open Spacing Closed Corners

So . . .

A wide open lip print suggests a person who is ready for anything! For this person, new ideas, perspectives, adventures and experiences are a necessary part of life. She enjoys action-filled days, stimulation, and fun and can be easily bored. The corners may be open or closed. If they are closed, as in Print 49, the sense of adventure will be tempered by caution. If they are open, (Print 50) she may not always think things through, may

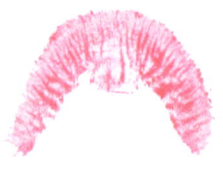

Print 50: Open Spacing
Open Corners

Print 51: Moderately
Open Spacing

Print 52: Narrow Spacing

be too spontaneous at times, and may find herself thinking, "What have I gotten myself into?" But she may also be someone who never meets a stranger, whose natural curiosity makes her genuinely attentive and inquisitive about new people, new ways of doing and new ways of being. Either way, she is flexible, adaptable, easy to get along with, and lots of fun!

The moderately open lip prints in Print 51 tell the tale of someone who is adventurous, but not fool-hardy. She's ready to cooperate with others and to explore all possibilities, and she's ready to have a good time. She is usually more easy-going and flexible than her tightly spaced friends.

Narrow spacing (Print 52) brings us into a more cautious mindset. She is still going to listen to your ideas, but will filter them through her own preconceived notions. She will listen less to you and more to her own inner guidance the narrower the spacing becomes.

Lips that are tightly closed suggest a cautious, careful, conservative mind-set. Jilly calls this a Missouri Lip Print, aptly named for "The Show Me State."

People who have this closed lip print (Prints 53 and 54) can be skeptical about the opinions of others, taking them with a grain of salt. They will want to do their own investigations, drilling down deep until they have discovered enough factual information to make wise decisions and choices. Missouri Lips will open to new ideas and experiences more easily if the ideas and experiences are their ideas! They can be stubborn, or at least tenacious about proving for themselves that a new thought or action is the right course to be taking.

Being cautious and careful, it's no surprise that these folks are the "Keepers of Traditions." They believe if it worked yesterday, it's worth doing it

Print 53: Missouri Lips

Print 54: Missouri Lips

again today. We can count on them to keep our traditions and pass them on to the next generation.

When we use the word conservative with regard to this print type, we are not necessarily referring to politics. Missouri Lips will defend their belief system, whether conservative or liberal, sticking by their beliefs until they have themselves discovered reasons to see things differently.

If this is you, you may have powerful defense systems in place to protect those beliefs and could be more sensitive and easily offended than someone with wider spacing.

There is beauty and power in being cautious and in keeping tradition alive. Still, seek to enhance your listening of an alternative point of view with more empathy. Be willing to consider the suggestions of others, as every now and then, you may hear something magical!

Varied or Consistent Spacing

Print 55: Consistent Spacing

When the spacing in a set of prints is consistent, as in Print 55, we have someone who is consistent in her demeanor, whatever her spacing. You always know who she'll be when you see her . . . no surprises. There is a comforting reliability to her way of being. If her spacing is narrow, as in the example, she is careful about what she believes and

Print 56: Varied Spacing

what actions she takes. Don't waste too much breath trying to change her mind about something. She's pretty sure she already knows the way it's going to be.

Or, you may see the prints slowly opening with each successive print, until the initial hesitancy dissolves into an attitude of, "Yeah! Let's do this!" The sequence of the prints in Print 56 suggests that this gal will relax into an experience, becoming more comfortable and spontaneous as she proceeds. She steps tentatively into the shallow end of the pool and moves towards full immersion in the deep end as she acclimates to the situation.

Or the reverse can happen when someone is initially enthusiastic, but wants to proceed with caution, as demonstrated in this set.

Print 57: Varied Spacing

In Print 57, the wide open print on the left was actually in the middle of the Kiss Card, and the two on the right were on the right third of the card. The position of print #1 on the left indicates that in the present moment she's feeling open and spontaneous. The print at the bottom shows more caution when her security is involved and on the right we see an exceptionally careful mind-set when critical decisions are being made about the future. A cautious and thoughtful approach would be expected of someone who has a "future tense" lip print that is sealed shut. Her husband explains it this way:

"When it comes to deciding important things, I'm all 'ready, fire, aim', and she's all 'aim, aim, aim'!"

For some of us, our minds and our sense of adventure may be opening and closing moment by moment. We expand and we contract. We relax and we tense up. We feel safe and in the next moment we feel vulnerable. This explains why we can see wide open and clamped shut lip prints on the same Kiss Card. (Print 58)

Print 58: Varied Spacing

What we want to now factor into our interpretation is the position of each print and the order in which it was made. In the set of prints above, we have someone who honors the traditions of the past. This is her most intense and her first position. She bases her daily decision making on time-honored beliefs. Further, she is extremely careful about making important decisions about the future, but she is willing and open in the moment to experience what is at hand.

Again, it is important to number the order of the lip prints. Where the lip prints are placed on the paper will give you clues about "where and when" the person is spending her time and thoughts. When you understand what the position of the print means you can overlay that interpretation on top of what may be surmised from which prints are open and which are closed.

THE SIGNIFICANCE OF CORNERS
THE DOORWAYS TO THE MIND

Personality Traits Displayed in Either or Both Corners

We can't talk about Spacing without talking about Corners. Let's look a little more closely at what corners say about a person.

If the eyes are the windows to your soul, the corners of your lip prints could be called the "doorways to the mind." Like doors, they open and close, allowing flow or barring the entrance of anything new or unexamined. Generally, corners speak to how thoughtful, careful or impulsive one might be. They also have to do with how one makes decisions, and how critical or insignificant due diligence is in any decision making.

Corners are one of the places where we see a sense of humor and how well someone can keep a secret. Do you hate surprises? It will show in your corners. Are you ready to get in the game and step up to the plate, or do you need a few practice swings first? Do you love to read? It will show in your lip print. Your corners are the "Deciders" of your lip prints. They are the funnels through which knowledge enters and where tradition and wisdom pull up a chair and get comfortable. When open, they channel the winds of change that blow through in continuous motion and renewal. When closed, they guard the gates of your privacy and discretion.

CORNER SPACING

Corners may be open widely, moderately, or just barely. There may be one corner open and one closed. The corners may both be closed. The meaning of spacing in corners parallels the meaning of spacing between the lips, and enhances or tempers the impact of that spacing.

Open Corners

We've talked about open spacing representing an open mind and a sense of receptivity to new concepts and undertakings. Open corners exponentially increase the willingness to try new things and to welcome change in one's life. Like spacing, the wider open the corners, the more impulsive and experimental the spirit.

Print 59: Wide Open Corners

Wide open corners show us that we have someone who can be fearless when encountering the unknown. She embraces change. When the corners are coupled with wide open spacing, she can be impetuous to the extreme. It's important for such a person to learn to stop, breathe, and consider the consequences when she feels herself being swept away by her own enthusiasm.

The gal in Print 59 may be ready to grab a bungee cord and jump off of a bridge! Such widely spread corners signal the owner to stop and think it over. Her mantra should be "Look before you leap!"

LIPSTORY | 92

Print 60: Wide Open Corners

Print 61: Moderately Open Corners

It's fine and fun, and worth celebrating to be willing to "go for it" with complete abandon in some situations, but developing a sense of discretion when you are this open is the wiser way to go. Knowing when to be impetuous and when to be cautious is part of the life curriculum for the wide-open-cornered person.

Having said that, there is another interpretation to wide open corners. The open "flood gates" may be less about the actions one takes and a desire for change, and more about an almost insatiable curiosity and desire to connect with new ideas and thought systems.

This is the print of a friend of mine, in Print 60, who is an artist and one of the most genuinely curious people I know. I have noticed over the years how truly interested she is in learning about others when she meets them. She asks questions I would never think of asking, and might not really care enough to ask about if I did. She is equally curious about her artistic boundaries and abilities, and has immersed herself in developing her skills, resulting in her success as an artist.

When your corners and spacing are moderately or slightly open, (Print 61) you are a person who is willing to allow change and who doesn't hang on to those things, thoughts or people who no longer serve or support you. Like a fresh breeze that blows through your life, your open corners represent your ability to release the past and welcome the new.

One Closed Corner

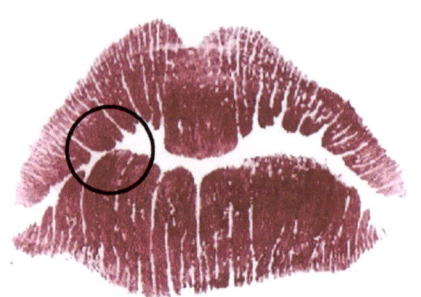

Print 62: One Closed Corner

A corner is closed if one lip has any contact at all with the opposite lip, or if there is even a speck of color attaching the two, as in Print 62 on the left side.

As we observed, open corners represent the ability to adapt to and even invite change and flow in your life. Again, think of each corner as a doorway. When they are both open, change and innovation are invited and welcome.

When one corner is closed and the other open, it represents a tendency for things, thoughts, or relationships to come in and stay, sometimes beyond their useful life. The stuff of life flows in the one open corner, and having nowhere to go, it gets backed up fast. There's no exit so at some point, like an overstuffed storage room, there's no space for anything new. On a material level, as well as emotionally, spiritually, and intellectually, we can get overloaded or blocked, leaving no leeway for growth or expansion. It takes energy to hold on to stuff that you don't need, and an abundance of fresh energy is waiting for those who can learn to let go!

One closed corner can signal that you enjoy collecting something specific. Maybe you collect art, or recipe books. You may collect friends or shoes or spoons. Look around your life and see if what you are holding onto is of value, or if you are perhaps a borderline hoarder! Your corner may be saying it's time to purge your closet, the garage, the attic or the top of your desk. It may be time to let go of certain people in your life. Take a look to see if there is a bit of over-accumulation going on materially, emotionally, or mentally.

The subject of attachment and practicing detachment fills countless volumes of teachings both in Eastern and Western spiritual traditions, and you can explore your own spiritual traditions for these teachings. If your lip prints are indicating attachment with one closed corner, you are being asked to examine your concepts regarding abundance versus scarcity and what that looks like to you.

Consider what are you overly attached to; so much so that it hinders and slows you down. It could be memories and regrets from the past. Or perhaps you hold on to old things for which you no longer have any use. If you are a pack rat with a garage full of sentimental "treasures," or a closet full of clothes that don't fit, or a desk full of unfiled paperwork, or shelves of books that you haven't read and will never read, remember that attachment is not just about clutter and disorganization in your life or the expense of storing and moving things that you don't need. It's not just about denying others the use of something they might really have need of, if you could just part with it. It is about scarcity consciousness and feeling disconnected from the abundance of an infinitely generous Universe. And that's where the work is.

Having one closed corner is an invitation from your higher consciousness to address your core beliefs about what it means to have and be "enough." Before you do any purging, take some time to go within in contemplation, prayer, or meditation. Sink into your inner depths until you meet the infinite quiet space within. Sitting in that space, in the presence of Sacred Thought, ask for clarity about what is really useful to you, and for the grace to relax into releasing the non-essential.

Both Corners Closed

When both corners are closed, you are the Queen of Caution. Closed corners show on people who do not like to be surprised in important matters. You may enjoy a surprise party on occasion, but when it comes to work, marriage, money, your possessions, and your future, you like to be in control of any decisions that affect you.

If your spacing is wide open, (Print 63) then you will be open to hearing about new ideas and adventures, but you will need to think it over and feel that you have enough information before you act on any new opportunities. You will listen with rapt attention to the car dealer as he tells you about all of the energy saving and ecologically friendly features of the all-electric car. But you will still drive home in your gas guzzler so that you can think it over, ask your Mother or best friend, and research the Internet to validate what you heard.

Print 63: Open with Closed Corners

If the spacing is tight, as in Print 64, then this need for caution and conservative actions will be enhanced even further. Especially if all of your prints are closed.

Print 64: Closed Spacing, Closed Corners

What you want to be aware of is that when you have closed corners, your tendency is to resist new ideas that you didn't originate. It is important to be thoughtful and to consider all sides of an issue before making an important decision, but carried to the extreme you may be overly hesitant to relax into a new experience or adventure that could bring you pleasure, satisfaction, or success. The need to control every aspect of your day doesn't leave much room for surprise and innovation.

If you have tightly closed corners, practice making lip prints with open spacing and corners, and notice how it feels to stretch yourself in this small way. If you would like changes in your life, such as a new romance or job, imagine yourself to be as "open as the sky" and see what opportunities present themselves to you.

A Few Last Words on Closed Corners

If you find that your corners are consistently closed, here are a couple of things to consider.

Closed corners are like closed and locked doors. A locked door allows us to sleep more securely at night. It means that we can leave our valuables and know that they will be safe from theft. On the other hand, we have each of us at one time or another been locked out of our home, office or car and felt the stress and inconvenience of the experience.

I hope that you have never been on the inside of a locked door without the freedom to leave, but being in prison is another way to experience a locked door. A closed and locked door is not necessarily a problem, but not having the key to open it at will is.

As we've learned, people with closed corners are generally more cautious and less impulsive than those with open corners. And thank goodness we have such people in the world to balance out the exuberant enthusiasm that has some of us chasing wild geese.

Due diligence and information gathering are valuable skills and provide a clear and essential service in the right situations. The ability to keep your mouth shut allows your work associates, your family and friends to trust that you will respect and protect their confidences. This is a rare gift in a world where every day internet commerce and social media threatens to divest us of the most basic forms of privacy and civility.

However, if you have closed corners on most of your lip prints, and especially if the spacing is tight, you may be locked into beliefs that hold you back or that shut out possibilities presented by others. Consider the concept of the fixed belief. A fixed belief is an idea that you hold as the truth that is not the truth. We all have such beliefs. They may be something like, "If I was a man, I would be able to make more money," or "It's hard for a woman my age to find a husband," or "There is only one way to this." Fixed beliefs are biases and prejudices that we don't question. They are misperceptions that we have picked up from our parents, our peers or teachers, from our religion or culture. They are the water that we swim in and so it is very difficult to discover them because we don't think to examine them. A fixed belief will often show up in our ideas about romance. "Nice girls don't do that." "I would never . . ." whatever that is that you would never do with someone you love and trust, if it doesn't harm anyone, is probably a fixed belief.

I met a woman whose daughter had married outside of her race and who had a beautiful granddaughter from that marriage. The woman told me that her ex-husband had never met their granddaughter because he believed that his daughter had sinned by marrying interracially. She showed me a picture of an adorable little girl who would never know her grandfather because of his bias against interracial marriage. This is what holding fixed beliefs will do. Like closed corners and locked doors, outworn convictions can hold you back from living a more expansive and self-expressed life. They are beliefs that separate you from others and shut down access to new corridors of maturation and evolution. They become prison bars that stop you, confine you and limit possibilities.

But you have the key to open those closed belief systems. Be willing to soften to new ideas. Outside of the corners that enclose your core beliefs is a world of infinite potentiality. Invite it in, a little at a time. Be willing to discover the ideas that are holding you back. Notice what you resist. Listen to your thoughts and when you hear the word "because" stopping you, see if what follows might be something the validity of which you could question.

We outgrow many of our fixed beliefs as we mature, but when your lip prints have closed corners, you'll need to dig a little deeper to find the ones that remain. They are worth discovering. The key to unlocking the doors and concepts that hold you back is simply in knowing they are there and pulling them open. They're only locked because they are not visible to you.

INFORMATION FUNNELS

An Information Funnel is the "V-shaped" channel at the corner of some lip prints. Like a funnel these openings concentrate the incoming "material."

They accentuate the already cautious and show a more investigative and studious nature than do prints that don't have them. If you see closed corners and Information Funnels in your prints, multiply your caution quotient by ten! The little horizontal "Vs" at the corners represent the channels that new ideas must work their way through before being granted an audience with your internal "decision maker." The longer the funnel, the more information is required for you to feel adequately informed.

Extreme Information Funnels suggest someone who isn't so much cautious, as he is an "information junkie." This is someone who will sit in front of his computer for hours researching the latest computer technology or the best place to stay on the Island of Samoa, reinforced by aerial views on Google Earth. Generally someone with long funnels loves to read or do research, and gather knowledge.

Print 65: Extreme Information Funnels with Open Corners

We may have Extreme Information Funnels with open corners. Here in Print 65 we see the print of a spiritual teacher who has committed his life to seeking wisdom and to exploring Universal Principles. He is a powerful and dynamic teacher, who has sat at the feet of a wide range of spiritual masters from Eastern Gurus to New Age thought leaders.

The Information Funnel on the left suggests the depth of information that he is willing to explore. Notice that his corners are open to the wide space between his lips. He is discriminating but willing, even eager, to entertain and be transformed by innovative spiritual concepts.

In Print 66 we see the lip print of my friend Amy, who is not going to like being left out of any decision-making process and who will perform her own due diligence to the nth

Print 66: Extreme Information Funnels with Closed Corners

degree. She's open-minded, but will need to feel in control of her environment. She understands what it means to take responsibility for herself and others. I knew her as a little girl. She was a studious child who made straight A's in school.

Amy is the mother of two daughters; one who was born prematurely and has had lifelong challenges. I don't have a better example of our so-called information junkie than Amy, nor a better way to illustrate what that means than to share with you her own words. Here is a transcript of her talking about her experience since her oldest daughter was born with disabilities.

> *"Meredith has opened my eyes to a whole new world. I did not know anything about prematurity and the seriousness of it. I, like everyone else, just thought premature babies were tiny and cute. Not so. They are often very, very sick and have lifelong health and learning issues. I didn't know that they have lung disease, hemorrhages in their brains, retinopathy, necrotizing intercolitis, holes in their hearts, apnea, cerebral palsy, seizures and/or meningitis. The day she was born, I began to learn a whole new vocabulary.*
>
> *Nowadays we see seven kinds of medical specialists. For years, we also saw an additional seven, for a total of fourteen. It seemed we lived in the doctor's office.*
>
> *Once I felt like Meredith was stable, I was called to help others in my shoes. I became a support parent for an organization call Family Connections of South Carolina. I helped them to learn the vocabulary, their rights and their responsibilities. I helped calm their nerves, and cried with them when despair set in. I also became the leader of a support group for parents of premature children. We named it HOPE.*
>
> *I served on the Advisory Council for Greenville Memorial Children's Hospital. We raised awareness and money for the children's hospital.*
>
> *As a family, we were the ambassadors for the March of Dimes in Greenville County. We spoke to employees of corporations and educated them on the importance of research treatments for premature infants.*
>
> *I learned about IEPs, accommodations, modifications, school until age 21, certificates of attendance vs. diplomas, self-contained classrooms,*

learning disabilities, IQ scores, and progress monitoring. I learned that my responsibility as a parent is to advocate for my child in all environments. It was important to know the law, and to insist that my child be given every opportunity to be successful in school.

As a result of wanting the best for my child, I became very involved in the schools. I served on the School Improvement Council as the secretary. I also served as secretary, treasurer and vice president of the PTA. I was the room mother for both of my children every year of elementary school. I found that if I stayed involved and volunteered at the school, not only did I know what was happening there, I could get whatever I needed!

Additionally, I served one year on the South Carolina Advisory Council for the Education of Special Education Students. This organization advocates for children with special education needs

School has always been an exciting place for me. I love children, and I have developed a passion for helping the underdog. I went back to school to become a special education teacher. The knowledge I gained from this degree not only got me a job that I love, it also gave me more insight into my daughter's mind."

Amy's comments go on: "If you happen to be disabled or have a chronic illness and a mental illness, you can just about forget being helped or treated. I found myself in a situation that I had to advocate for my child once again. As a result, I have addressed members of the South Carolina congress at rallies. I have written many letters to members of our congress. I have sent messages via email and Facebook to directors of hospitals. I don't accept that mentally disabilities make people ineligible for appropriate and adequate treatment!

I am now serving as the secretary for the Barbara Stone Foundation. It is an organization that raises money to provide services that Medicaid and the department of disabilities do not provide for people with disabilities. I continue to learn about resources and the lack of resources every day!"

Amy is an excellent example of someone who has a thirst for information. You can see how as she learned about one thing, she turned and built on that knowledge time and again until she was in a position to speak with authority to people who could affect change. That skill of digging down, deeper and deeper and mining for knowledge is the innate gift of someone with Extreme Information Funnels. Maybe they should be called Information Shovels!

Amy and Meredith

INFORMATION EDDY

I named the Information Eddy after Jilly Eddy (not because she has one, but because she deserves to have an indicator named after her). The circular space inside of the Information Funnel acts as a vortex or an eddy that catches information and spins it around and around. If you have an Eddy, you will sometimes overthink things in an obsessive way. If the Eddy is on the right side, as in Print 67, you will have difficulty making decisions about the future. If it is on the left side, as in Print 68, you'll spend an undue amount of time rehashing the past. Here's a "righty" and a "lefty." Print 67 actually belongs to a lawyer. It may serve his clients well that he spends so much time ruminating. On the other hand, his round and round thinking may slow him down in his personal endeavors, as if he's caught in a traffic circle with no exit!

Print 67: Information Eddy on the Right

Print 68: Information Eddy on the Left

Print 69: Information Eddys

Print 69 is one that shows Information Eddys on both sides of the print, with closed funnels sealing them in. This man is another lawyer, a partner at a large law firm in Phoenix. Again, it would appear that his rather extreme proclivity for over-thinking things serves him well as a lawyer. A lawyer can channel his ruminations towards winning a case. In another person however, this kind of inner churning of information could be debilitating. It's important to move forward and to release the pent up energy stored in the Eddys.

We won't always have time in our readings of others to move deeply into such subjects as the dynamics of decision making, but if you do see an Information Eddy, if someone is having a difficult time making a decision, reassure the subject that she has the ability to gather the information needed to make good choices, and that the fear of making a decision is a decision in itself. As Yogi Berra said, "If you come to a fork in the road, take it." Any choice you make will break the inertia of indecision and create the forward momentum you need to find your way.

ZINGERS

It would be a boring world to live in without Zingers! These pointy, sometimes needle sharp corners which can be found on both the upper and lower lip, are a hallmark of those who shoot from the hip verbally. When something needs to be said, this is the mouth that's going to say it! The more extreme the pointy-ness, the more compelled the owner of the lips may be to offer unsolicited suggestions or to find fault. Difficulty with tact is often, though not always, a characteristic of those sporting these saber-like protrusions. If you grew up with a pointed tongue, you have probably learned by now to be more careful. Your verbal barbs may often be softened by a playful wit.

Print 70: Softer Zingers

Print 71: Round with Zingers

Print 72: Square with Zingers

Print 73: Triangle with Zingers

Print 74: Motivational Speaker with Zingers

Zingers are in fact one place that your sense of humor will show up in your lip print. If the Gourmet Lip Split represents your heart humor, your Zingers represent your mental wit. You could think of Zinger wit as "humor with an agenda," your way of motivating people to do things your way.

When the Zingers are less pointed and more rounded, (Print 70) your comments will be softer and less aggressive. They will be offered with less attachment to the outcome of your suggestions.

We see Zingers frequently on round lip prints, (Print 71) suggesting the motivational and goal-oriented aspect of that shape. The Round person wants to keep things moving forward and will use her words to verbally prod people in the direction she would like them to move so that goals and timelines can be met.

On the square Problem Solver (Print 72), Zingers represent the direct-approach-guidance offered by one who is solidly rooted in a sense of purpose and responsibility. If you ask a Problem Solver for help, and he has Zingers…brace yourself for the no-nonsense solution that is coming your way!

The Diamond and Triangle showing Zingers (Print 73) are the motivational speakers and mentors whose no-excuses verbal nudging moves others towards the discovery of their own talents and abilities.

Zingers are neither bad nor good. They simply represent a style of expressing oneself. I have seen them on gifted teachers (Print 74) who are known for speaking the truth in ways that jolt others into consciousness. But if your Zingers are sharp, take care. Sarcasm likes to sneak into those sharp corners like a coiled snake ready to strike!

I'VE GOT A SECRET!

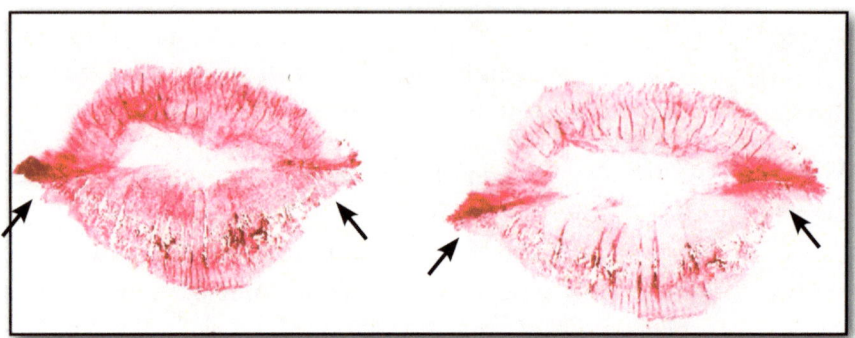

Kiss Card showing Energized Corners

Corners are sometimes dark in color, indicating added energy. When you see energized and closed corners on a lip print, like these two, it may indicate that the owner has access to confidential information and he is clamping down on it with vigor! He is not about to allow it to escape. He may be a lawyer or a counselor. Maybe he handles medical records or is a banker.

The energy lines showing here could also mean that he is holding on tightly to information that he would rather not have, or that he doesn't know what to do with. Finding a suitable way to relieve the stress of guarding this secret without betraying the trust that has been placed in him would be important.

On the other hand, he may just be someone who keeps a confidence very well. He can be trusted with a secret, as it will take a crow bar to pry anything out of those well-guarded corners!

BLINDERS

When one or both sides of the lip print are either faded or missing, we are looking at the indicator called Blinders.

Blinders are your lips' way of telling you to slow down and take a breath! Often, when you have Blinders, you are someone who hits the ground running in the morning holding a list of things to do. You spend your day moving from task to task, checking things off of the list. Blinders suggest that your tasking takes precedence over everything and everyone else. Errands, laundry, grocery shopping, getting the kids dressed and fed, making dinner, or completing whatever else is on the list becomes the most important thing. Your missing corners disguise the reality of whether you are happy or sad. Who can tell whether your lips turn up or down at the corners? You're too busy to know yourself!

Blinders indicate a focused mind, but it is a stressful focus. Stress depletes and distracts you from the moment and interferes with your productivity. Blinders further suggest that you have become disconnected from yourself and others, from a sense of your own "being," and are now fixated on "doing." What would you see and experience if you were not so absent from the moment?

You might see a husband, a child, a parent, a friend or a co-worker who would love to have more time with you. You might realize that you have lost touch with the big picture of your life and ceded your days to an unconscious, Zombie-like attachment to getting from point A to point B.

When visible, your corners may be open or closed. Open corners say that you would welcome change in your very busy life, if you knew how to create it. Closed corners say you are too busy to understand how much you need a change!

Blinders are a very loving message coming straight from your heart to YOU! You are being reminded of what is important. You are being invited to stop, relax and reconnect!

Now is a good time to consider putting yourself on your daily list of "to-dos," and to make the list shorter. It's time to step back, breathe deeply and relax. Focus without relaxation is not the most effective state of being. You'll be much more productive if you move through your chores, errands and tasks with attentive serenity.

Schedule some time for yourself without the list. Set aside a day, an afternoon, or a couple of hours for yourself. Go to a spa, or sit in your backyard alone. Unplug for a few hours from your phone, social network, iPad, or laptop. It's time to check in with yourself and with your dreams. Take some time to do an assessment of the four levels of "dreaming".

Sit quietly somewhere where you will not be disturbed and try this exercise:

Close your eyes and allow your personal dreams to come into your thoughts. What are your desires, goals, wishes and hungers? What unfulfilled ambitions do you hold that are achievable if you could find the time and resources to go for them? What steps could you take to forward those dreams?

Next imagine your personal vision expanding outward to include the people around you. How do your dreams involve your family, friends, co-workers and acquaintances? How can you forward these goals toward manifestation in the collective around you?

The third level of dreaming is the planetary level. Can you imagine your personal and collective dreams extending out into the world at large? If money and resources were not an issue, what would you dream for the planet, for the environment for all sentient creatures, for this world that gave you physical life? How could you give back some small fraction of the blessings the world has given to you and to all of your ancestors?

Finally, consider your immortal dream. What lasting legacy would you like to leave when you are gone? As martial arts actor and legend Bruce Lee said, "The key to immortality is first living a life worth remembering." Never be afraid to reach for a grand vision in your life!

Make a commitment to your dreams. Gather your attention for part of each day around your deepest desires.

A daily practice such as yoga, meditation or prayer will assist you in staying aligned with your desires and goals. Be productive, but do so in a conscious way. When you are relaxed and intentional your tasks are more fun. You become more accessible to yourself and those you love. Tasking turns into "goal tending" and dreams are pulled into form in present reality.

HAPPY OR DROOPY?

Don't Worry, Be Happy

You may have noticed by now that some lip prints look happy and some look sad. Many are all business and don't seem to convey a mood. For those that do, the ones that strike you as happy indicate an optimistic and a "glass is half-full" kind of character. Some lip prints just look like a smile, and will bring a smile to your face when you see them!

When the corners are upturned and open, you have someone who is generally upbeat and open to change. He likes to be busy and entertained and gets bored easily. If the corners are closed but turned up, you've got a happy person who is content with the status quo and is feelin' groovy.

Droopy Lips

Lip prints that seem sad are showing you a pessimistic nature. They may not always be extreme Gloom and Doomers, but they will lean towards that side of the room.

If the corners are open and turned down, you're looking at a person who is not feeling great about things and believes he would welcome positive changes in his life. Unfortunately, with a propensity to "see through a glass, darkly," he may not feel any better about things even when they do change.

If the corners are closed and turning down, and if they are yours, part of your challenge, part of your work, is to cultivate a consciousness of gratitude. This applies even if your corners are open. When we are feeling depressed or dissatisfied, it is because we are living in the energy of "not-enough." I recently read this provocative statement in *Faith and the Placebo Effect* by Lolette Kuby. She wrote, "Don't ask God for anything. He has nothing more to give you. He's already given you everything." Open your mind, heart and yes, your corners, to the stream of Life. Practice being grateful for everything that you have, are and experience. It is impossible to be in a negative state of mind and to be truly grateful at the same time.

Take responsibility for your attitude, for your mind set, for your internal experience of living. You are the one creating your contentment or discontentment. No one else has the power or capacity to stand inside your mind and make you feel happy or sad. Even though it's tempting to blame others or your life situation for your pessimistic viewpoint, in reality, barring a neurological disorder, you are powerful enough to decide how you feel and how you respond. Practice saying "yes" to all that exists in your life, accepting your present circumstances for what they are. A gloomy outlook will deplete you of energy, making it more difficult to change the things you would like to be different. The bad news is there's no one to blame for how you see the world. The good news is you have complete and utter control over how you see it. Choose happy.

BFF ~ BEST FRIENDS FOREVER

There's an interesting indicator that shows up now and then. I call it the **BFF** (Best Friends Forever) indicator. It sometimes looks like a smaller lip print within a larger lip print, as it is caused by the inner edges of the lip prints being darker than the outer edges.

Sometimes the upper outline will be wider or narrower than the lower outline. Or there may only be a dark outline on one of the lips.

When you see darker color in this way, it indicates that the person is feeling protective of her feelings. The dark color represents a barrier that holds people at a distance while she takes the time to assess their place in her life. As she speaks and interacts with others she feels vulnerable, so she lays down this emotional line of protection which shows as the BFF Line. The line on the upper lip represents her need to protect herself in any public forum . . . to take care before allowing others to know her in more than a social or superficial way. The line on the lower lip represents her need to protect her inner feelings and thoughts, her private responses to the world around her.

Together, the lines represent her inner circle, into which she will be slow to accept new people. She must come to believe that others can be trusted not to betray her before she embraces them as friends. However, once that happens, she's there for the long haul as a long-term trusted and loyal friend. The BFF knows what true friendship is and you can count on her to be there when friendship matters.

IMPORTANT FEATURES OF THE UPPER LIP

CUPID'S BOW

Our lips and our prints, for those of us who sign our Valentine's Day cards with them, are subjected to a beauty standard that is as rigid and subliminally implanted in our cultural psyche as the allure of thin, young and large-breasted bathing suit models.

The most beautiful lips and their resultant prints, as perceived by makeup artists, fine artists, cosmetic companies, modeling agencies, plastic surgeons and Madison Avenue, are full and voluptuous things with a perfect Cupid's Bow. The Cupid's Bow (Print 75) is found at the apex of the top lip.

Print 75: Apex of the Lip

Named for its resemblance to the bow of the Roman god of love, this feature comes in a variety of sizes and shapes, some shallow, some wide and sloping, some cut deep like a crack in a rock, (Print 76) and of course the model-perfect ideal that resembles the top of a Valentine heart (Print 77). In spite of a prevailing bias that perfect lips have this feature, only about 25% of the lip prints I have collected actually display a Cupid's Bow.

Print 76: Narrow Cupid's Bow

In reality lip prints, like Cupid's Bows, come in a wonderful assortment of shapes and sizes, with rounded tops, bumpy tops, flat tops and every combination possible.

Print 77: Classic Cupid's Bow

But for now, let us consider the Cupid's Bow. The first thing to know is that not every valley or "V" on the upper lip line is a true Cupid's Bow. To determine whether you are looking at the real thing, draw a line along the upper lip line and across the area where the valley is. A genuine Cupid's Bow dips down into the upper lip, forming a white space below the line, as in Print 78. If the valley is above the line, you have People Movers, which I will discuss later. (Print 79)

A Cupid's Bow cuts a wedge, a scoop or a crevice out of the upper lip, intruding into the heart of the lip. It is an indentation that creates space for outside entry, like an airlock on a space station or the foyer of your home.

Print 78: Cupid's Bow

Print 79: People Movers

The owner of a Cupid's Bow is someone who allows another person's opinion, like an invited guest, to penetrate into her personal space. She makes accommodation for and opens the door to someone else's feelings, point of view or needs. It matters to her what another person thinks and feels. She is empathetic, the negotiator, the person who will consider the other's position before making a decision. She seeks the win/win solution for everyone. She may further invite another's opinion to come in and stay. She may decide to keep that opinion for herself, virtually "adopting" this guest.

This is not to say that there are only 25% of the general population who will negotiate. Lots of us will sit down and listen to what other people need, propose or demand. Some will do so with a preconceived idea of what the end result will be, but owners of a Cupid's Bow are actually willing to budge and will do so without having to adhere to an inflexible agenda. Many of us will go through the motions, but are not quite as sincere about giving ground as the personality of this persuasion.

Another quality of this print type is that she is someone who cares about making a good impression. Well-groomed and often artistic in her self-expression, she delights in putting her best foot forward at every opportunity. She hungers for balance and fairness, and if the bow is deep, she will sometimes give too much away in her desire to create the "win" for others.

Because of this, the deeper the bow, the more likely we'll see situations wherein she will allow herself to be negotiated out of things that are important to her. Although the owner of a deep Cupid's Bow will at times surrender her position in the interest of fairness to others, and do so willingly and with generosity of heart, there may be other times when giving way could engender resentment and anger on her part. Like the volcano that the "V" reminds us of, an eruption can happen suddenly and lay waste to anyone in its path!

If you do have a deep Cupid's Bow, your message is to learn to stand in your integrity, and be willing to ask for what you need. Hold on to what is rightfully yours, whether it's money, your way of doing things, your principles, or your heart. Negotiate . . . the world needs you. Be willing to consider the wants and needs of others, but not at the expense of sacrificing what may be vital to you. Like the Problem Solver of the square lip print, the Cupid's Bow wants to consciously empower all involved through her negotiations.

Then "V" will be for Victory and authentic self-respect.

SMOOTH~TOP

The lip print with no Cupid's Bow, but with a smooth top that is either round or flat on the upper lip instead, is the print of someone who is unique and who desires autonomy. He does not like to be bossed around by others. Do not try to micro-manage a Smooth-Top.

He's just not very interested in how you would do it. You will be wasting your breath if you offer unsolicited advice or your opinion to a Smooth-Top person. He may be polite enough to listen and may even thank you for taking the time to share your thoughts (depending on the fullness of his upper lip). But then, after you walk away, he will do it the way he'd intended to before you offered your opinion.

Smooth-Tops are independent thinkers. With open corners, they are creatively adventurous and with closed corners, they have a carefully cultivated style of their own. Left to do a job, they will do it well and efficiently without outside direction, as they know what works for them and what doesn't. And if they need help, they'll ask for it.

Sometimes I read the lip prints of children, and naturally, some of them have this lip print type. Print 80 belongs to a five-year-old girl. As you can imagine, it's tough for a Smooth-Top child to be told, day in and day out, how to behave and what to do. Even though our children need to learn from us and other adults, it's a challenging prospect for a "mavericky" kid. If you have a Smooth-Top child it's wise to consider the built-in, natural resistance she will have to following orders. Give her credit when she does so and seek ways to allow her to express her originality. When she's impatient, help her channel her expression in creative and positive ways.

Print 80: Child's Smooth-Top

Remember that you are blessed with a child who has the potential and desire to make her own way in the world.

If you have this feature, you know how much you dislike being managed, and how important it is to you to be allowed the freedom to find your own voice.

Learn to flow with the suggestions of others without creating an irritated or judgmental response internally. Not everyone will understand that you are such a self-starter. Allow others to be who they are, even if it appears they want to tell you what to do. Relax into non-judgment. Let their suggestions be spoken, and don't be afraid to surround yourself with mentors who can offer good ones. Be willing to check in to see if any of the ideas of others are useful, and let the rest flow around and past you, as you continue on your autonomous way!

PEOPLE MOVERS

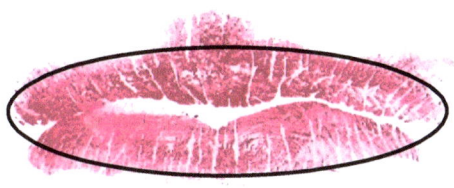 

A People Mover is a bump that protrudes from the top of the upper lip. It can easily be mistaken for a Cupid's Bow, when there are two of them. Let me describe how to tell the two indicators apart.

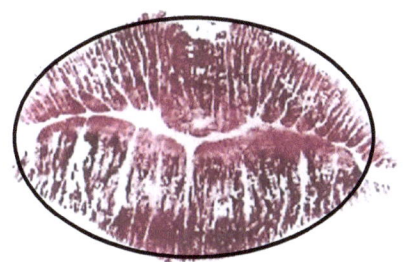

Print 81: Cupid's Bow

The true Cupid's Bow cuts down into the upper lip line, as you can see in Print 81. In Print 82 we see that People Movers sit above the lip line, like little mountain peaks. They are an expression of reaching out and extending oneself. They denote ambition and leadership. Someone with People Movers is not afraid to ask others to follow her lead. She will also have high expectations of those who do.

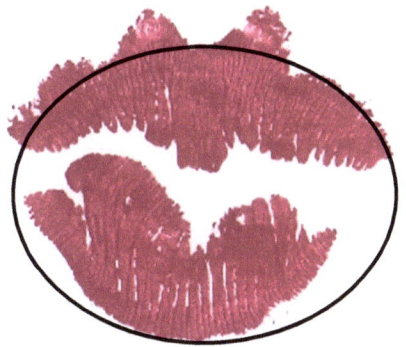

Print 82: People Mover

Sometimes there will be half of a Cupid's Bow and the other side will be a People Mover. (Print 83) In this case, there will be a combination of the desire to find a win/win and the need to direct the outcome. Just like the owner of the Cupid's Bow, the People Mover is a negotiator, but she is less likely to compromise what's important to her.

There is another type of People Mover that is the "dromedary" of apexes, "the single hump" People Mover. This may appear to be a Smooth-Top, but

IMPORTANT FEATURES OF THE UPPER LIP | 115

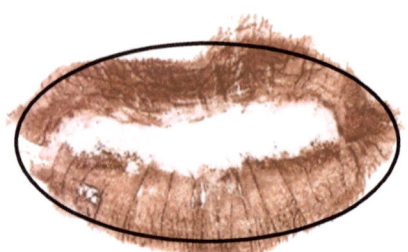

Print 83: People Mover

if you look closely and follow the line of the upper lip, you'll see that the middle of the lip rises above the lip line. (Print 84) Again, we would read this as a People Mover with Smooth-Top characteristics.

People Movers are leaders. In the appropriate situation, where they have authority, their ability to speak up and take action is a valuable factor in their success. If you have a People Mover, you would rather tell others how to do things than be told yourself. One must be willing to direct others if one is to lead, teach, manage, or be the boss. However, in some situations you may be perceived as just downright pushy, so this leadership indicator should be used with restraint and discrimination! Moms, managers, teachers, and corporate leaders who are used to being listened to may have to soften their approach in their personal and ancillary relationships.

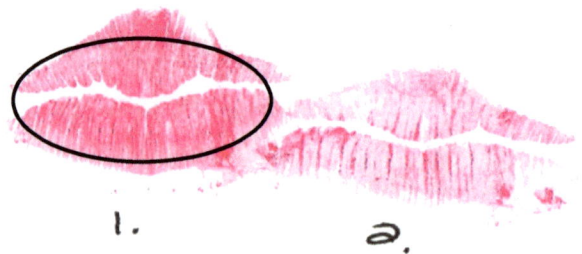

Print 84: Dromedary People Mover

People Movers are ambitious. The desire to extend oneself fearlessly out into the world is a beautiful and powerful attribute that can propel People Movers to great success. If you have a child with People Movers, when she is testing your limits and wanting things her way, remember what Sheryl Sandberg, the former COO of Facebook, and author of the book *Lean In,* says about female empowerment. "We have to stop telling our little girls that they are bossy and start telling them they are leaders." Little boys with People Movers might like to hear the same.

Underneath every People Mover is a desire to excel and to make a difference. Those of you with this indicator would do well to make peace with that desire, and to acknowledge your own efforts, as well as those of others. Celebrate your accomplishments, and find the time to give praise to those you manage, lead or teach. Lead with integrity and compassion, and make a difference that matters!

THE HUG PUCKER

Print 85: Circle of Romance

The Hug Pucker is located in the center and on the lower edge of the upper lip. It is the top half of the Circle of Romance, which consists of the Hug Pucker (1) and the Gourmet Lip Split (2).

These two indicators, positioned at the core of the lip print, have the most to say about our closest and most important relationships.

The Hug Pucker, big surprise, is one of the central indicators of our affectionate nature. It stores information about our relationships, and also suggests how much affection we are likely to feel that we need from others. It indicates how well we are communicating with those to whom we are close.

The Gourmet Lip Split, which will be discussed later, indicates how passionate a person is and how ready she is to indulge those passions. Individually these two indicators cover a broad range of characteristics displayed, but together they paint a picture of the romantic nature of a person.

A prominent Hug Pucker may hang in the middle of the lip like a stalactite. Or, it may be a full fleshy orb-like thing, often with creases or white lines on either side defining it. Some lip prints don't have this fullness, but rather appear to be flat in the center of the lip.

There are three categories that a Hug Pucker can fall into. They are:

    The Cuddly Hug Pucker

    The Recessive Hug Pucker

    The Flat Hug Pucker

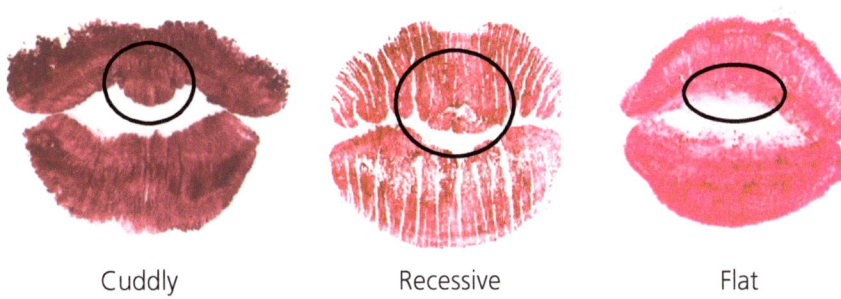

Cuddly   Recessive   Flat

IMPORTANT FEATURES OF THE UPPER LIP

The Cuddly Hug Pucker

Small Cuddly   Medium Cuddly   Large Cuddly

The Cuddly Hug Pucker is identified by following the inner line of the upper lip from corner to corner. If in a set of lip prints, the Hug Pucker consistently dips down below the lip line like a stalactite hanging from the ceiling of a cave, especially when there is a good amount of space between the lips, then you have a Cuddly Hug Pucker. Some Cuddly Hug Puckers will be more prominent than others, but what they have in common is that they don't go away from print to print.

As a reader of lip prints, you must take into consideration whether the Hug Pucker is small and slightly visible, medium sized and moderately visible, or large and prominent.

In general, and at best, the expression of the Cuddly Hug Pucker is one of open-hearted love. This is Granny rushing at you with her arms wide open and a huge smile of approval on her face. This is your friend's face lighting up when she sees you. Or, imagine standing on a stage and receiving a standing ovation from a cheering crowd of people who love you. That's what it's like to be with someone who fully expresses the Cuddly Hug Pucker. She will be present and loving with you and you will always feel affirmed in her presence. If you are romantically involved with a Cuddly Hug Pucker, lucky you! With your Cuddly Hug Pucker, whether she's a bit shy or as bold as Whoopi Goldberg, there is room for a deep and nurturing heart connection. She can be loyal to a fault.

There are nuances to how the Cuddly Hug Pucker is expressed. The slight Cuddly Hug Pucker is often found on people who love in a quiet way. They are not ostentatious, nor do they crave attention from strangers. They are generous with their hugs and affection if you are a friend or family, otherwise they will hold back and probably be inclined to shake your hand rather than hug you on your first meeting. They are often uncomfortable with public displays of affection. But don't be misled . . . the Cuddly Hug Pucker can be very passionate when you get her alone. She is romantic, a bit idealistic, and warm-hearted.

Moderate Cuddly Hug Puckers are warm, and as advertised, very cuddly. They will be hand holders who enjoy snuggling on the sofa, stealing a kiss in public, and slow dancing. Your response in kind will be welcome and anticipated. If you have a moderate Cuddly Hug Pucker as a partner, romance is an ever present possibility!

Prominent Cuddly Hug Puckers will desire more attention than less pronounced ones, whether it comes in the form of a hug, verbal praise, or applause. They are born performers and enjoy being the center of attention and the life of the party. They often have great charisma and find it easy to attract a following of admirers while they vie for your attention by entertaining you with a story, a joke, or a song. They may not ask you directly for the hug they are craving, but give them one anyway. If you see this Hug Pucker on a child, be sure to shower him with hugs and affirmation often.

Sometimes the Cuddly Hug Pucker is expressed as a need to be self-affirmed by claiming the spotlight and stealing it from others. Since the slight Cuddly Hug Pucker is a bit shy, this is more likely to happen with a prominent Hug Pucker.

If this is you, learn to ask for that expression of love; the hug, the kiss, the affirmation. Don't expect others to read your mind. You have a naturally loving heart, so let your affection flow and wash over those around you.

The Recessive Hug Pucker

The Recessive Hug Pucker seems to be more common than the Cuddly Hug Pucker. It usually has a parenthesis of white lines or dark energy lines defining it on either side.

Small Recessive   Medium Recessive   Large Recessive

It may be hanging below the lip line, but in some prints it will draw up into the lip line and be even with it, like a turtle pulling its head inside its shell. Often when the mouth is open wider, it will recede and become flat, unlike a Cuddly Hug Pucker which will still remain evident with the mouth open.

The size of the Hug Pucker can be slight, moderate or prominent, so take into account the degree of prominence or size of the Recessive Hug Pucker and amplify or decrease the qualities of the feature in your assessment accordingly.

The Recessive Hug Pucker is as capable of being affectionate and cuddly, and as romantic and passionate as the Cuddly Hug Pucker. The main difference between the Recessive Hug Pucker and the Cuddly Hug Pucker is that the former can be reclusive or moody sometimes, with a need to withdraw from others. Your Recessive Hug Pucker girlfriend may draw a circle around herself and say, "I need this space and time for me! You're all on your own. You know I love you, now go away." A prominent Recessive Hug Pucker may be someone who craves attention, until she doesn't.

When we are dreaming our dreams and goals, we need to go within and it's important that we have the autonomy to do so. If you know someone with a Recessive Hug Pucker, allow her the time she needs for introspection or regrouping. If you are such a person, be firm about designing the schedule and quiet time that you need for yourself, but do it with kindness, with understanding and compassion for others and their needs. It's important that you remember that others may feel shut out when you, like a hibernating grizzly, retreat into your den.

Remember to tell your friends, family, partner and especially your children how important they are to you and how much you love them. Tell them often; more often than you think is necessary. Others love to hear it, and even if you think they should know . . . people forget.

The Flat Hug Pucker

Flat Hug Puckers

Sometimes the center of the upper lip is flat as a pancake. There's no visible evidence of any protrusion in that area. This is still going to be the area that you look at to see indicators regarding the person's close relationships.

When the Hug Pucker is flat, we have two possible interpretations.

In the first case, this person can be very loving and affectionate without being pushy about it, and her family and friends will have no complaints about how she shows her love. But still waters run deep with the Flat Hug Pucker. In romance, she may be feeling strong emotions under her quiet demeanor, along with a healthy sex drive, but she'll show finesse and restraint in how she expresses her desires. She can be a very smooth operator!

On the other hand, our **Flat Hug Pucker** may not be getting the attention she would like, but she is able to distract herself with work, play or friendship for now. Below the surface, the desire may still there, but she carries herself with composure and apparent patience as she fills her time with non-romantic endeavors.

If you have a Flat Hug Pucker, behind that air of restraint beats a loving and passionate heart. Watch out for those distractions that take you away from your true desires. Work on relaxing into the moment, pump up your spontaneity, and find ways to connect your creative and passionate aspects to the relationships that are in front of you right now.

THE MOTHER HEN

Print 86: Mother Hen

Print 87: Mother Hen

This indicator always gets a laugh when I interpret it, because the person with the indicator knows that I have hit the nail on the head. When the upper lip extends out past, down and around the lower lip like the wings of a Mother Hen sheltering her baby chicks, we have someone who is a natural at taking others under her wings and caring for them. This is your girlfriend who adopts stray animals, or who volunteers at a senior center. She spends time offering advice, helping with chores, or loaning money to the "less fortunate." She may be a social worker, a nurse, a teacher or a corporate leader. She has a huge heart full of compassion, but she has expectations of her charges as well. She may be the very organized team leader who keeps everyone on a cohesive path forward, or a busy mom who manages to keep everyone bathed, fed and dressed for school. She is protective of those she loves and will guard them in times of danger. She may overdo it sometimes.

Print 86 belongs to the administrative director of a non-profit spiritual education organization. Her nickname is "Mother Superior." Print 87 belongs to a woman who started a large, successful networking group that supports hundreds of small business owners in marketing themselves to potential clients.

And last, Print 88 belongs to a spiritual healer and teacher. Along with her husband, she is the matriarchal leader of an international organization that teaches Native American wisdom. She has no problem disciplining her students and expects the best from them . . . just as their mothers would.

Print 88: Mother Hen

IMPORTANT FEATURES OF THE LOWER LIP

LOWER CUPID'S BOW

The Diplomat's Indicator

The Lower Cupid's Bow is the indentation we see here in the center of the lower lip. Whereas a Cupid's Bow on the upper lip represents a propensity to empathize with others, to seek approval and to negotiate for the win-win, the lower Cupid's Bow represents a negotiation with oneself. Part of that negotiation has to do with how you will show up in your communications with others and what your strategy will be.

When you have an upper Cupid's Bow, you are eager to negotiate a harmonious outcome for everyone and to maintain an even keel in your relationships. When you have this negotiating indicator on your lower lip, but not on your upper lip, you will enter any sort of mediation having already negotiated with yourself about what the best course of action is. You want balance, you care about the outcome, but you have given yourself a "primary directive." You want it your way. You will steer the ship of discussion in the direction of your own true north.

This is a beautiful blend of the two diverse intentions of the Cupid's Bow and the Smooth-Top. It's a powerful and usually winning position to take in the world of diplomacy. Imagine a female Secretary of State negotiating for peace in the Middle East, and you will understand the power of this indicator.

It's not uncommon for a woman with a lower Cupid's Bow to have been raised with brothers or to find herself working in a male dominated environment. If this is you, with your stance and determination, you will appear to be tougher than you may feel sometimes. You may seem to show up as more masculine, energetically, than you believe yourself to be. But this determination and toughness is not a façade. Women with a lower Cupid's Bow are well connected to their "inner warrior" or their inner masculine side, without sacrificing their feminine side. This is a good thing, not something to shy away from. In our quest for balance, it is wise to recognize and accept the yin and yang of our being. A woman with a Lower Cupid's Bow is a force to be reckoned with in a Man's World.

Print 89: Lower Cupid's Bow

For a man who has a lower Cupid's Bow, this indicator points towards his inner "female warrior." These men can also be emotionally expressive, and may cry more easily than other men. A conscious connection to the inner warrior brings us pure intentions, focus, organization and relaxed authority. When a man is aligned with his inner warrior, we see his ability to stand in serenity in situations that require a presence of power without aggression. In a woman, we see a confident, grounded and assertive leader. But she always has a softer side and can go there when she is not in a situation that asks her to be so unshakable.

Print 90: Lower Cupid's Bow

When you have an upper and a lower Cupid's Bow you will have great skill in diplomacy. Thin lips show your skill with analyzing every aspect of a situation as you prepare to negotiate. The fuller your lips, the better you will be able to charm others into agreement.

With both the Upper and the Lower Cupid's Bow, you will be empathetic, seeking the best course of action based on the desires and highest good of all parties while maintaining your integrity in the process.

PERSONAL PUSHER

Extreme Personal Pushers

Moderate Personal Pushers

The **Personal Pusher** looks like a bump on the bottom edge of your lip. It may be large or small, but if you have a personal pusher on your lower lip, you have set a very high standard for yourself. You are deeply motivated when you set out to accomplish something. Even those closest to you have no idea how important it is to you to succeed. Try to remember this, because when you do accomplish something, no one else will be able to appreciate what you have achieved as well as you can. No one else knows how important it was to you, what it meant to you. And even if your friends, your partner, your family, and your associates all acknowledge you, you will not feel fully satisfied until you acknowledge yourself for the job you achieved.

Know that you will always be driven to go for the gold. Relax into your self-identification as a high achiever. Embrace your need to do your best and most importantly . . . don't hold back when it comes time to give yourself a pat on the back!

If your Personal Pusher is accompanied by a Lower Cupid's Bow, you will have very high expectations of yourself in any negotiation. If your work involves bringing consensus (as most work does) you may find that you are deeply attached to outcome and that you take it hard when things don't go the way you hoped. This would be an invitation to practice non-attachment. Do your best, and be willing to accept the results of your efforts.

POINTED BOTTOM

Pointed Bottoms

The **Pointed Bottom** is a little different from a Personal Pusher. When the lower lip comes to a point, there is a high degree of focus and drive. This indicator shows creativity and a strong will, especially when it completes the diamond shape. Coupled with a Smooth-Top or People Mover, the pointed lower lip will push forward with intensity, regardless of any naysayers. Her ambition and strong opinions may be more evident to those around her than someone with a Personal Pusher.

Like the Personal Pusher, the pointed lower lip can reach high goals, but must stay sensitive to the dreams of others caught in the wake of her enthusiastic forward motion. When the pointed lower lip is the lower half of a diamond shape, it's imperative for the owner of the lips to remember that others are looking to her as a role model and leader . . . and to carry the mantle of mentorship with responsibility and compassion.

ROUND BOTTOM

Round Bottoms

A rounded lower lip indicates a people person. This is someone who is affable, generous, and compassionate. She wants others to be as happy as she is. It is often the lower half of a round lip print, which carries the qualities of kindness, going with the flow and making others comfortable. There is the possibility in this type that the person will be overly self-sacrificing so as to be seen as important to others. With the rounded lower lip, we have someone whose nature is to put others first and she may have difficulty thinking of and caring for her own welfare. She is social and enjoys group activities. She's a team player and needs to feel connected to others. Naturally other indicators such as zingers will factor in, but in general, the easy going round lower lip brings with her an attitude of congeniality and helpfulness.

CENTER STAGE

Center Stage

There is an additional lower lip feature that is worth learning about.

IMPORTANT FEATURES OF THE LOWER LIP

Sometimes you'll notice that the bottom lip is wider than the upper lip. This can be understood as the opposite of the Mother Hen indicator, which is all about fussing over and protecting others. When the lower lip is wide, subjugating the upper lip, the person can seem to be self-centered. His lip is saying that, "It's all about me!" He wants to be the focus of attention. I used to avoid speaking about this indicator to these happily unaware people. I wasn't sure how to say to someone "It's really all about you, isn't it?" The funny thing is, someone with this lower lip would probably laugh and say, "Of course it is!"

This is the ego on hyper-drive. This person will always turn the conversation back to himself. As that old punch line goes: "Enough about me, let's talk about you. What do you think of me?"

Over time I began to understand that an extremely egocentric perspective may also be a temporary condition. There could be a momentary trauma causing the person to be self-absorbed as she processes the situation. If someone is battling a disease, or dealing with a loss, or trying to understand an insult, it's reasonable and human for her to be engrossed by her own needs.

One day I did a reading that taught me that a wide lower lip can actually hold another diverse but related interpretation.

One night I had the opportunity to read the lip prints of a man who teaches about human behavior and personal development. On that evening I heard him speak with great inspiration about his life and how he had come to study the words and works of the world's greatest philosophers. He spoke of the years he spent applying these universal truths to his own life experience. It is from this point of self-awareness and with great humility and no pretense that he now takes the stage and spotlight to share what he has learned with others.

When I saw his lip prints, I realized that the wider lower lip can indicate someone who uses his personal experience as a platform from which to teach others how to find their own pathway to success. Rather than teaching the words of all of the philosophers he studied, he teaches how he has applied those words to create the life he is now living. He is the true expression of someone who stands center stage and says, "Listen and learn from my example, from what I have discovered and lived. I am here to share with you that you too can absolutely fulfill your own dreams."

This is the light-filled side of the feature. When you see it, don't assume you have a self-absorbed person in front of you, although that's possible. And even if that interpretation holds true, it may be that the person is going through some-thing in the present that is causing some understandable self-obsession. On the other hand . . . you might be looking at someone who could bring profound transformation to the lives of others if he only knew it were possible! And you may be the one meant to tell him.

THE GOURMET LIP SPLIT

Print 91: Gourmet Lip Split

The **Gourmet Lip Split** (GLS) is located in the middle of the lower lip on the upper or inner edge. In a print, it looks like a "V" if it is prominent, or it may show as a line, or two or more lines, that mark the center of the lip.

The qualities that go with a Gourmet Lip Split include a deep appreciation for food and/or a passion for cooking and entertaining, a romantic, sensual or sentimental nature, a sense of humor and a beautiful laugh. A GLS doesn't always indicate that the owner loves good food. She may be a lover of junk food, but you can expect that food will definitely be a source of pleasure to the GLS wearer and that food will play a big part in the social scene of the person.

The owner of a Gourmet Lip Split enjoys the good things in life and will be someone who is happiest when her surroundings and belongings are pleasing to her. She gives her appetites permission to be indulged and has the capacity to enjoy all of the pleasures that life can offer. The GLS is one half of the Circle of Romance, and a prominent GLS indicates a passionate nature. She may not be a cheap date, but she'll be worth it!

A Gourmet Lip Split likes to entertain, sharing laughter and conversation with people she enjoys around a table of food and drink. She is social, charismatic and easy to love, and will attract fans just being herself. She'll remember special occasions and do her best to make them even more special by adding her naturally creative touch.

Having a Gourmet Lip Split, doesn't necessarily mean that you will overindulge in food, but that's a possibility. Or you may find yourself too attached to having "things." Addictions of any kind would be an expression of the "unconscious" side of the Gourmet Lip Split.

The Gourmet Lip Split qualities will show up in subtle or conspicuous ways in direct relationship to how subtle or extreme the indicator is.

Print 92: Subtle Gourmet Lip Split

If it is subtle, such as in Prints 92 and 93, we have someone with a refined, sophisticated sense of humor, and an elegant and casual touch when it comes to entertaining and enjoying food. She will usually enjoy cooking and/or eating in a good restaurant. She may have a collection of gourmet cookbooks. The owner of the lips on the left below has a melodious laugh that sounds like bells tinkling in a breeze. It's important to her to have a lovely, well decorated home. When she gives a dinner party, it is a healthy and creative dining experience.

Print 93, with just a fine white line defining his GLS, comes from a man who has a TV show about travel and unusual regional foods. He has a subtle but quick sense of humor and will eat anything once!

Print 93: Subtle Gourmet Lip Split

Prints 94 and 95 are two examples of an extreme GLS. These two people are born comedians. In fact, the one on the left is a professional comedian who worked at Universal Studios in Florida when we met. The example on the right was someone I met at an event who was an outrageous flirt and had me and everyone around us laughing out loud with his humor and upbeat personality.

The fullness of the lips will always enhance the qualities of the GLS, the degree to which one indulges one's appetites and the subtle or outrageous expression of passion and a sense of humor that is irrepressible in our GLS friends.

Prints 94 (left) and 95: Extreme Gourmet Lip Splits

MULTIPLE GOURMET LIP SPLIT

Multiple Gourmet Lip Splits

Sometimes you'll see a **Multiple Gourmet Lip Split**, as in these two examples. This is the ultimate and amplified expression of all of the qualities and attributes the GLS represents. The owner of this indicator will have a great appetite for food, romance and life in general. Fasten your seat belt, because she will take you on a joyful pleasure ride, laughing all the way!

The print on the left is a gorgeous, willowy, bright and personable Spa Sales Director at a resort in Paradise Valley, Arizona. Let's call her Gabrielle. Her GLS is subtle. The resort she works at is one that U.S. presidents have stayed at, so, you can imagine a work environment that is quite luxurious. Gabrielle is the perfect liaison between the spa and the clientele who frequent it. She is perfectly groomed, manicured and expensively dressed. Popular among her work associates, I have often seen her at elegant resort events, interacting with the "beautiful people" who frequent the hotel. Her ready smile is radiant and is as genuine as her charisma. From all appearances, Gabrielle has been graced with all of the talents and attributes a woman needs to attract a luxurious lifestyle.

The print on the right comes from a woman I met several times at the Spa of this resort. She was always greeted warmly by the technicians in the beauty salon of the spa, signaling to me that she was a frequent client and someone everyone admired. I remember being astonished by her beauty. The expensive clothing, jewelry and accessories that she wore were the best quality. She is, like Gabrielle, visibly blessed in life not just in the physical and material aspect, but also in the spiritual, mental, emotional and passionate aspects. My conversations with her revealed the presence of a deeply engaged woman who is seeking to grow in wisdom, who has a generous nature and who carries a true passion for living an extraordinary life.

You can count on having a good time with your GLS friends, and if romance is on your mind, your GLS partner will be an enthusiastic participant.

If you have a Gourmet Lip Split, and even more so if you have a Multiple GLS, it is yours to own that you have the ability to draw into your life, the people, things and circumstances that bring you pleasure. Know, as well, that you bring pleasure to those you enjoy being with in ways that come very naturally to you. Charisma, baby!

LOWER HUG PUCKER

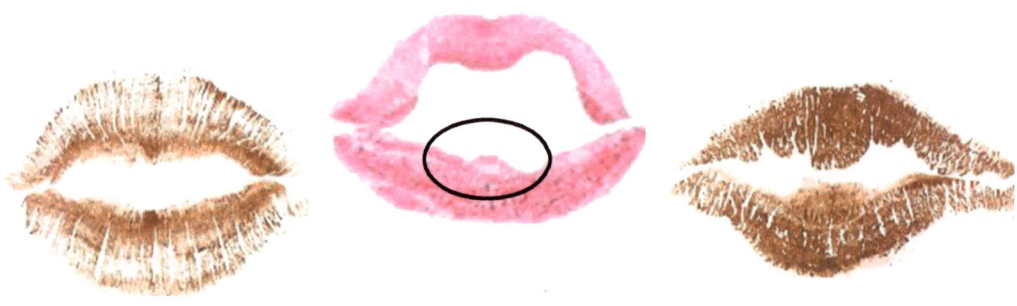

Lower Hug Pucker

The **Lower Hug Pucker** is an indicator that you may see in the area of a Gourmet Lip Split. It looks like a protrusion rising up where the GLS would be. It may be a bump or simply an energized area, as in the print on the left above. When you see this indicator, you are looking at a person who is in need of a hug.

But most of all, this person needs to give herself a hug. She may have a tendency to compensate for the love she wants to feel for herself by over-indulging her appetites, whether it's eating, shopping, sex or doing whatever satisfies and soothes her. Once again the subtlety or extremity of her over-indulgence will be demonstrated in the size or intensity of the indicator.

I believe that the Lower Hug Pucker as an indicator has more to tell us than we presently understand about it, so if you see one, ask gentle questions and see what you can discover. Then ask for a hug!

GENERAL COLOR INTENSITY

Cheerleader Lip Prints

Cheerleader Lip Prints

Lip prints, being the 2 dimensional things that they are, can offer us three basic properties to study. They have color, they have shapes and they have location . . . the location of the print on the Kiss Card, the location of the feature or indicator and the location of the color or the missing color. Let's turn our attention to color: missing, faded or intense.

In a lip print, color equals energy, so the three lip prints above represent what we call cheerleader energy. I love this quote I found by a young cheerleader:

"Fly high, do or die, dare to dream, cheer extreme."

Kara – Cheerleader, WC, Ohio, USA

This quote from a champion cheerleader says what you can expect from someone with dark, solid color in their lip prints. A Cheerleader Lip Print tells you that this person has enough energy and charisma to excite and motivate those around her. She's a persuasive and compelling leader, engaging others in her interests and causes through her sparkling enthusiasm.

If color is energy, then missing color means energy is missing. When examining a lip print, we look at the overall quality of the color. Is it faded, moderate, or intense in color? Are there lines or bands of missing color? And where in the lip print is the missing or intense color? For example, a squiggly line of missing color on the upper lip means something different than a squiggly line on the lower lip.

Print 96: Intense Color

Print 97: Intense Background

Print 98: Faded Background

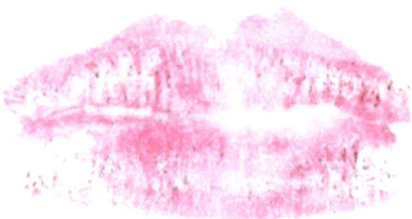

Print 99: Mottled Background

So color and its intensity play a major part in the translation of the message in a lip print. When we look at a print, the color may be solid and dark as in lip Print 96.

Or the print may be generally dark with indicators breaking up the field of color, resulting in lessening its intensity, as Print 97.

The background color can alternatively be moderate or pale, with indicators further lessening the color value, as in Prints 98 and 99.

Color Equals Energy

When we see the color intensity as energy, we begin to get a sense of the overall energetic condition of the person who made the print.

The next step is to determine if the energetic loss is physical or if it is being initiated by one of the other energetic bodies; the mental, emotional, spiritual or passionate/creative systems. From there we can discuss ways to stalk, recapture and reintegrate the energy that has gotten away from us.

Look at the set of three prints on the kiss card in Print 100. The first shows moderate energy, the second less than moderate and the third shows low energy.

You may ask, "Isn't that just because the lipstick wore off while the prints were being made?" Well, yes and no. Yes, it did wear off. But no one said that the person making the prints couldn't reapply her lipstick before making each print.

Next is a Kiss Card that a friend of mine made for me. (Print 101)

Print 100: Fading Intensity

She reapplied without any direction from me. The level of energy that shows here is a true representation of her energetic levels. She is the lead singer in a 10-piece band, she tours internationally with another world famous singing group, she is head coach of her son's football team, and is an avid racquetball player, in fact a past state champion. Her physical energy is intense! She's optimistic, healthy and always upbeat. People who reapply are usually people with very good physical energy and health. If they ask me if they can reapply, I just say, "If you want to, go ahead."

Print 101: Cheerleader Intensity

Still, if you look closely you'll see the same missing color in all of her prints along the lower edge of the lower lip. You'll also see a horizontal band across the upper lip, and a little color missing in the Hug Pucker. The missing energy is definitely not originating from the physical body, but instead from one of the other four energetic systems. In reading these prints I would affirm her talents, energy and power, and gently explore what her missing color is pointing her toward.

As I have mentioned before, there are exceptions to the rule of "missing color equals missing energy." Those exceptions include Spiritual Lines and indicators of potential and purpose, and will be explained in Part 2 of this book.

In addition, we will explore the five energetic bodies that present themselves in our lip prints, and we will look at how we can use our energetic indicators as guidance in our quest for a greater understanding of who we are and why we are here.

In every moment our lip prints are registering our moods, our health, our emotions, our thoughts, judgments, concerns, worries, passions and our distractions. Our spiritual connections, our ability to cope with stress, or to stay present . . . all of this energetic information displays in our prints and is waiting to be deciphered and considered as we progress on our journey of life and living. I look forward to sharing much more with you in the next part of this book.

Part 2

The Energetic Indicators

ESSENCE AND ENERGY

In Part 2 of this book, we veer away from the personality traits and dive deeply into the psychological and spiritual aspects of lip print reading. We will look at what these indicators suggest, and I will share with you my observations and experiences with regard to how they may be seen as guidance. Because the science of lip print reading is sparsely explored territory, my inquiry has been solidly based on the lineage of interpretation that I learned from Jilly Eddy, seasoned with a distillation of my spiritual influences and intuition, and blended with the feedback that I have received from my clients.

I bring my personal understanding of Truth to my study of lip prints, and into the essence of each reading . . . and so will you, in your own way. An intuitive reader can find heart-to-heart connection with the person being read and still stay true to the messages in the lip prints without diminishing the convictions of anyone involved.

Make no mistake . . . this is a spiritual journey and Lip Print Reading is about transforming the heart and mind. Whatever your beliefs are about God or the existence of a Universal Intelligent Consciousness, I think most would agree that there is an intangible dimension from which we receive inspiration, creative thoughts, insight, vision and the voice of wisdom whispering in our minds. This dimension permeates our lip prints in ways that push us beyond our comfortable patterns and beliefs.

Pam at Work

From another perspective, Lip Print Reading is energy work. When we look at a lip print, we see visible clues regarding the essence and energy of the people we read, and we are in a position to inform them in ways that are helpful and even healing.

When I am hired to do readings at a party, I know that I am being hired to entertain. Many of my clients think of me as a "fortune teller," and I will not have fulfilled their expectations if I am not amusing to their guests.

But when I hold a Kiss Card under the light, what I am really doing is holding a space for transformation for both of us. If you have the opportunity to read another person's lip prints, you must do so with the utmost respect. Whether she knows it or not, she is allowing you into her personal field of energy and her innermost way of being. As you interpret the wisdom teachings that are in the lip prints of others, you begin to own that wisdom yourself in ways you hadn't imagined. You begin to feel the blessing of the messages as much as the subject does. You will have moments of revelation and you will see the same happening in your subjects . . . perhaps not every time . . . but often. So keep it light and entertaining, but remain mindful of the possibility for insight and inspiration that your readings may offer another.

Color Equals Energy, Usually . . .

There are exceptions to every rule. The rule we learned in Part 1 was: Color intensity in a lip print equals the intensity of energy in the person . . . specifically in each of that person's energetic bodies. So, if color equals energy in a lip print, intense color equals intense energy and faded or missing color equals weak or missing energy.

But every rule has its exceptions, and so does this one. There are specific indicators that show as missing color, but actually signify no loss. Instead they are symbols of power or support, of talents and skills or of open receptors that are being fed energetically. We'll point out the exceptions later, but in general, the rule usually rules! Most faded energy indicators suggest that energy is being lost in one energy body or another, often because we're just not paying attention.

Let's look at these energy bodies.

There are many different ways to define energy, but when I read a lip print I am looking for indicators that speak to these energetic systems:

Physical - the body's vitality, health, and well-being

Physical Indicators show as "background" color, from solid to faded.
There may be splotchy or mottled color, or dots, or missing parts.

Mental - the thoughts and beliefs of the mind and the ego

    Mental Indicators are lines.

Emotional - the physiological and psychological response or feelings that result from thoughts

    Emotional Indicators show as bands or areas of fading or intensity.

Spiritual - our connection to Divine Consciousness

    Spiritual Indicators show as lines, dots, stars, wedges and wings.

Passionate/Creative - our passion and desire to procreate, and our desire to create with our imagination and artistic abilities

    Passionate/Creative Indicators show as areas of faded or intense color or in the outline of the print.

Each of these energetic bodies is interdependent on and interconnected with the others. As a whole, they make up what might be called our Luminous Being.[xi] When one energetic system is depleted, the others will be affected . . . yet if we can think of each separately it will be easier to direct our focus toward the recovery of lost resources.

Your Personal Utilities

In our homes we have running water, electricity, gas, cable connections, and phone service. Having access to these utilities makes our home and our lives more comfortable. On a cold morning we get up, turn on the lights and turn up the heat. After a hot shower, we blow-dry our hair and make a hot breakfast. If we awake to a power loss simple things become substantially more difficult. We count on, even take for granted, these resources in our daily lives, and we manage these resources by turning off the lights and faucets and saving energy when we can.

Just as your home has resources, or utilities, the energy bodies of your Luminous Being are your personal resources, your personal utilities. Whether you are talking about your home or your own luminosity, your utilitarian resources require careful and intentional management if you are to be at your best and most energized.

Imagine turning on all of the faucets in your home; the bathrooms, the kitchen, the laundry room, the outside spigots, and then letting them run all the time. And then, imagine what your electric bill would be if you left your thermostat on 65 degrees all summer.

We all know better ways than this to manage the resources that come into our homes. We know that if we waste our resources, it will cost us. Many of us like to think that we are environmentally conscious enough to respect these resources and to recognize the value of them by conserving energy when we can.

But, even if you "think green" and are always looking to reduce your carbon footprint, it's very possible that you are guilty of wasting your personal energetic resources every day.

Mental distraction, worry, regret, anxiety, judgment and stress are all ways that we waste mental and emotional energy. Each time you allow yourself to wander out of the present moment into the imaginary land of a fearful future or regret for a past event, you are running up an energy bill that's going to cost you. When you indulge yourself in disappointment day after day, your personal faucets are all turned on full force and your resources are metaphorically and literally flowing down the drain.

Those of you who spend your physical energy all day without any thought to earning and banking energy to replace what you are spending will find yourselves in energetic debt sooner or later. And if you ignore your spiritual and creative utilities, you may find that they have been "disconnected" when you weren't paying attention.

We want to be conscious of each of our energetic bodies. Learning to read the messages in our lip prints is an invaluable way to monitor what's getting away from us. The beauty of our lip prints is how specific the indicators are. Whenever we are losing energy, all of our being will be impacted, but if we can target the origin of the loss, we can set our intentions on stopping the loss at its source. This is the power and purpose of reading lip prints. We can see specifically which body is losing energy and we can target our attention on that energy leak, stalk the energy, and recapture it . . . because it's ours and we have a right to the use of it.

If your basement were flooding from a burst water pipe, the first thing you would do is turn off the water main to the house. You'd go to the source of the flooding. In a similar way, if you are exhausted from an emotional disappointment, taking a nap will only help so much. Your disappointment will continue to deplete you physically and must be dealt with before you can feel the energy flowing in balance again. Your lips will tell you where to begin.

Get connected on a gut and heart level to how much each of these aspects of yourself contributes to your well-being as you move through each day. Be grateful for each energy body and give it the care and attention it needs to be there for you. Just as you care for the home you live in, the car you drive, the clothes you wear, learn how to take good care of your body, your mind, your emotions, your spirit and your passions. Develop a sense of respect for these resources and honor them for the treasures and gifts that they are. They are endowments, so learn to spend them wisely.

We stand a good chance of finding peace and fulfilling our life purpose when we are attentive to managing each aspect of our energetic resources. Listen to the messages in your lip prints. Allow them to lift you out of fatigue, depression, stress and confusion into the higher realms of clarity and serenity.

THE PHYSICAL INDICATORS

When we look at a lip print, we are looking at a printed record of the energetic system of the individual person as it was in the very moment that the print was made. Regarding the physical energy, we are looking for three basic indications:

Color intensity and fading: Is the color solid and intense, or is it faded or mottled in its coloration?

Peppering: are there dark specks in the upper or lower lip?

Missing parts and asymmetry: Is the whole lip print there, or is part of it missing?

Let's look at each of these factors.

INTENSITY AND FADING

We learned in Part 1 that a bright, mostly solid lip print is called a "Cheerleader" print because it represents someone with powerful physical vitality and a positive mental and emotional attitude. When you see this in a print, as in this example on the left, you may compliment the person on her stamina and sparkle and move on to other indications. If you see depletion, represented by faded color, showing in the second and third print, this will be a strong indication of something other than physical fatigue or ill health.

Print 102: Cheerleader Lip Print

When we see depletion (fading of color) in a lip print, (Print 103) the first thing we want to discern is which energy body is the primary source of the depletion and, thus, the one we are first called to speak about. We may see that there is missing energy, but is the source mental, emotional, physical, creative or spiritual? If we're not sure, we can usually discover the source with gentle questioning. When you have read a few lip prints, you'll begin to see the difference between fading that is primarily a physical depletion, and fading that is coming from another source.

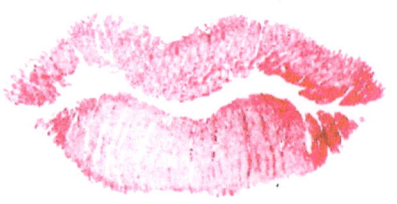

Print 103: Depletion of Energy

With a person who is low on physical resources or just tired, the fading will usually show in the first lip print and will continue to fade with each subsequent print. It is gradual and consistently weak and generally mottled or splotchy. There may be other depletion indicators, representing a loss of mental or emotional energy for example, but there will be a strong need for that person to rebuild the physical so that the other aspects can be pulled back into balance.

We see extreme depletion in the set of prints shown in Print 104, such that we can barely see the third print. There are other factors here that are showing depletion, but I would address the lack of physical resources as the first priority when deciding where to start with the reading. It is important to focus on recapturing the lost energy source of the physical in order to have some solid ground to stand on when addressing the other depletions.

Print 104: Extreme Depletion

The set of prints in Print 105 belongs to an 84 year-old woman. Notice the mottled coloring in the first print, and then the fading in the next two. If we think of a set of three prints as tracking how much energy we start our day with and what we have left at the end of the day, we can see that our subject doesn't have much to begin with, and accomplishing even small goals will be a challenge. You will often see this kind of physical depletion in older subjects, people who are ill, and in anyone who is not managing their "Jing" well.

In Chinese medicine, Jing is one of the "Three Treasures."[xii] It is the life-force energy that we inherit at birth from our parents and ancestors, and includes our ability to regenerate physically. As we age, we lose Jing, and although we will eventually run out of it, we can nurture and replenish our supply of Jing when we manage our energy resourcefully and with respect for the gift that it is. We can learn to stop the

Print 105: Extreme Depletion

practices that deplete it and redirect wasted energy into our energetic reserves so that we regain and experience what the Chinese call "radiant health."[xiii]

The kind of mottling we see in the set in Print 106 is always an indication of physical fatigue. It is the opposite of Cheerleader energy. It may or may not also be coupled with emotional depletion, possibly chronic low grade depression or disappointment and pessimism. Another cause may be a lack of self-care, such as poor diet, addictions,

Print 106: Mottled Lips

lack of sleep, or even anemia. We'll see it in chronically ill people, but by no means does it necessarily mean the person is ill. Still, when we are energetically deficient, our immune system will be more easily challenged, so there is merit in focusing on taking care of oneself with increased diligence.

If you have this kind of depletion in your prints, it's time to find ways to earn energy and to bank it during the day. Your lip prints are calling you, rather overtly, to seek high-grade nutritional support and to increase your hydration and exercise, it may no

THE PHYSICAL INDICATORS | 147

longer be enough to rely on being restored by a night of sleep. Quality sleep is still vital, but more must be done to gather and store Jing. When the depletion is this extreme, the energy must be replenished and reserves built in order for one to have the resources to accomplish goals, or even simple tasks.

Mottling asks us to look for ways to schedule an oasis into our afternoon. You might call it a mini-Mediterranean vacation. Our culture doesn't support the Mediterranean practice of having a leisurely lunch with family or friends, followed by a 2 hour nap before beginning the rest of the day refreshed and rested. But how about taking 15 minutes to a half hour in the afternoon to rest or meditate, or to take a brisk walk, or to spend time with someone who makes you laugh?

Listening to up-tempo music and singing along can help some people. Whatever gets your energy moving again, whatever stirs your blood and inspires you would be a good way to start rebuilding your reserves of physical energy and shining some light on your mood. As we get older finding ways to earn energy in the daytime is important to our health and longevity. Think of it as building an energetic savings plan.

NON-PHYSICAL FADING

If the first lip print is strong and the next ones show bands of fading, the depletion will often be more emotional than physical. Look at the set above. The first print is powerful and intense, with a little fading showing on the upper and lower lips towards the inside. That fading spreads in the second print and washes over most of the third. The physical power of this person is evident in the first print. She's healthy and vivacious. But the source of the fading that we see is originating on some level other than the physical.

In Print 107, we see the solid first print at the top where the subject "blotted" her lips on the edge of the Kiss Card. She then followed with two prints that would be invisible if not for the outlines.

Print 107: Non-Physical Fading

In Print 108, we see a powerful first print with lots of physical energy present, but some major fading in the second print. All three of these examples show us non-physical fading. We'll talk about the causes of the fading we see in these prints later, but for now, start to get a feel for how to distinguish the difference between physical depletion and non-physical depletion.

Now look at the print in Print 109. When there are many minute indicators causing fading, such as the multitude of white lines in the upper and lower lips seen here, and yet the background color is strong, the root cause of the depletion, as in the previous examples, will not be physical.

Print 108: Non-Physical Fading

Print 109: Non-Physical Fading

THE PHYSICAL INDICATORS | 149

INNER RESERVES

Print 110: Depleted Inner Reserves

At times you'll see depletion showing in the lower lip but not as much in the upper lip . . . or the opposite may be true. So let's look at that.

In our first example, Print 110, the lower lip shows a great deal more fading than the upper lip. Here is someone who puts on a brave face and pretends to have more stamina than she actually has. She will agree to do more than she feels up to and pay the price later. She may be wearing uncomfortable shoes, but she's smiling at the camera! Or, she's the mother who cleans the house and cooks the holiday dinner, scrubs the dishes and then says, Sure! Let's go to a movie, when what she really wants to do is crawl into bed.

With this indicator, the upper lip represents the face we show to the world, and the lower lip is our inner self, which in this case is running on empty!

Print 111: Inner Reserves

Our next example (Print 111) shows someone who may be flat out on the couch after a day of work, but if her friends call and invite her to go out dancing, she'll put on her dancing shoes and fly out the door. She appears to be on her last leg, unlike our holiday Mom, but she has a well of untapped inner resources that she can draw on when needed. However, the depletion is real. The upper fading is still a call to protect and restore those inner resources to prevent her well of available energy from drying up.

Sometimes you'll see a set of prints like the one in Print 112. When the person's third print is intense, with or without a reapplication of her lipstick, it means that she gets her second wind in the evening. She has enough true inner resources to rebound and to be ready for the evening activities.

Print 112: True Inner Reserves

PEPPERING

Peppering in a lip print looks like someone took a pepper grinder and sprinkled the lip prints with it. Peppering can be found in the upper lip (See Print 113a) or in the lower lip, as in Print 113b.

Upper Peppering, or dark specks in the upper lip, are not a physical indicator, so we will leave them for later when we get to the mental and emotional indicators.

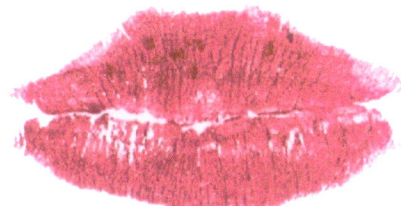 

Print 113a: Upper Peppering

LOWER PEPPERING

When you see Peppering (dark flecks of color) in the lower lip, this is a signal from your body that you are in need of some self-care. It may be that you are just overtired, or that you are dehydrated. Or it may be something more. Often when I mention this to my clients, they already know what is causing the imbalance. Whether a person knows what's amiss, or she just knows that something is up with her body, her lips are asking her to take care of herself and to do what needs to be done to recover her well-being.

Print 113b: Lower Peppering

MISSING PARTS VS. ASYMMETRY

We just looked at how to gauge inner reserves, so when you see the set of prints in Print 114, you should know right away that the subject has powerful inner reserves triumphing over the outwardly apparent lack of physical power. But there is something more going on here.

Print 114: Missing Parts and Inner Reserves

In prints number 1 and 2, the upper lip is nearly and actually missing! In print 3 we see missing parts again, most evident on the left side, top and bottom. (Be careful! Don't mistake an asymmetrical print for one with a piece missing.)

It is indisputable when you meet her that this woman has significant physical challenges, which are the result of a stroke. Her left arm and leg are affected, as evidenced by the missing left side of her print number 3. We see some of the right side of print 3 missing as well, indicating that that side has been affected by the disability she now faces.

You would not expect her to have the reserves that she does, based on appearances. But she is always cheerful. She never complains, and she is socially active . . . showing up to the degree that her level of mobility allows. She has never given up on life despite the challenges she faces every day. Her inner reserves, which are in powerful evidence in her prints, drive her to get out of bed and face each day with optimism and a smile on her face, despite the enormous effort it must take. She is upbeat and loving and a real inspiration. I am one of her biggest fans!

Here are two more examples of prints with missing parts. The lip prints in Print 115 belong to a man who was recovering from an injury to his right knee, and Print 116 is the print of someone who had recently had surgery on his right knee.

Print 115: Missing Parts – Knee Injury
(Arrows Indicate Missing Parts)

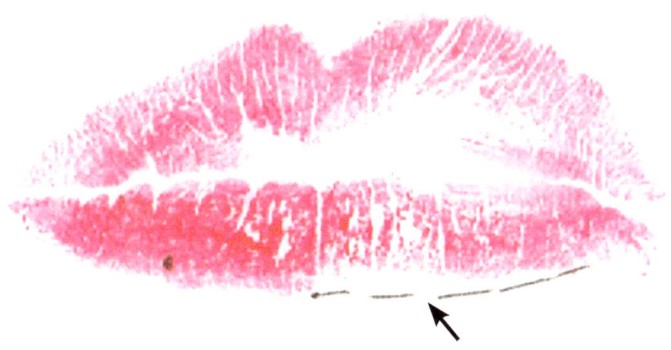

Print 116: Missing Parts – Knee Injury

In the context of health indicators, a missing piece of the print suggests trauma, injury, or illness. We saw missing corners when we learned about "Blinders" in Part 1, but this is something different. If I'm unsure whether I am looking at Blinders or at a missing piece, I ask the subject which interpretation applies to her.

A clue to determining if there is a missing piece of the lip print is to look at the symmetry of the print. Does the right side match the left side? Or is there a chunk that's gone, as in print number three? There are **asymmetrical** prints, also known as **irregular** prints, but a missing part is a chunk missing from a symmetrical print.

That brings us to the question of what we can learn about health issues in a lip print.

LIP ANATOMY MAP

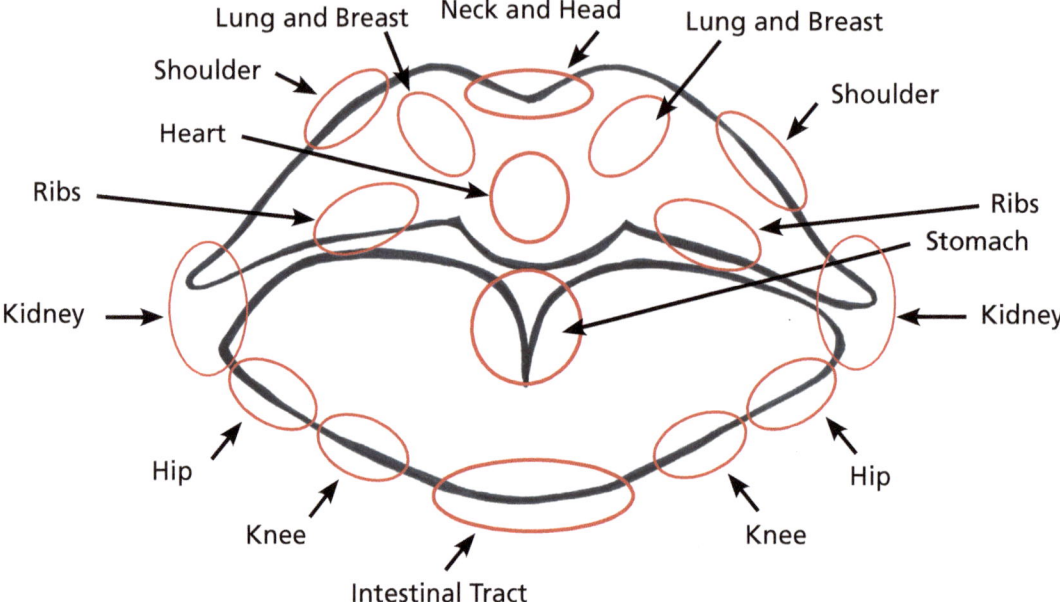

In this "Anatomy Map of the Lips" you'll see the areas that I have identified in actual readings as representing particular parts of the body. Please remember that this information is anecdotal and has not been properly researched. I'm sharing some of the feedback I have gotten in readings so that you have some idea of how physical trauma can display.

As we have seen, illness and trauma will often show as missing parts, or as peppering, fading or intensity in the lip print. Note that the upper lip represents the body above the waist and the lower lip represents the body below the waist. Injuries above the waist will show in the upper lip, right, center and left. Injuries below the waist will show in the lower lip, right, center and left. I hope you have noticed by now that lip prints are not a mirror image, but an exact reflection, and that the right side of a lip print correlates to the right side of the body.

At one event, the hostess asked me to give her a reading. I saw something in her prints on the right side in the area I have labeled "Ribs". There was color missing so that the pattern looked like half of a ribcage. When I asked the client if she was having any problems with her ribs, she looked at her friend and they both looked surprised. "I can't believe this," she said. "I have two broken ribs!"

Print 117: Missing Parts

Let's revisit the lip prints of the 84 year-old woman. (Print 117) You'll see a missing part of her upper lip, on the right, in print number 2. These prints were made after the woman suffered a fall that caused a hematoma in her right breast. The missing part is on the upper lip (above the waist) and on the right side of the body.

We also see a missing part of the lower lip in the Gourmet Lip Split area of prints 1 and 3. The subject also has chronic digestive problems. Think of these missing parts, and missing parts in general, as a loss of Jing Energy . . . a substantial depletion that should not be ignored.

The challenge with lip prints and health indicators is that the trauma indicators are inconsistent. They don't show in every lip print. It seems that our lip prints offer the messages they want us to hear on any given day, and information about our health is only one of many possible messages that we find.

Here is one more example of a health indicator. (Print 118)

A friend of mine broke her arm and I didn't see her for several months while she was recovering. When we finally got together for lunch, she gave me her lip prints and the one in the position of the past (1) showed the injury to the upper right side of her body.

She had recovered by then and her other two prints (the present and the future) did not show the trauma of the break, suggesting that she was fully recovered and had moved beyond it.

Print 118: Broken Right Arm

More research needs to be done in this area, and we must be very cautious when talking about health. If you are doing a reading for someone, you may have an opportunity to explore an indication of illness or trauma, but always as a cautious inquiry, **never as a diagnosis**. Let me know what you discover!

MENTAL INDICATORS

Print 119: Mental Indicators

Mental Indicators show as lines in the upper and lower lips. The lines may be white, missing color, or they may be dark and energized. Simply put, thoughts and mental activity show up as lines.

Let's take a look at this thought machine we call our mind. We understand that we think thoughts and receive knowledge with our mind. There is no doubt that the mind is a fantastically useful tool that has extraordinarily creative abilities . . . but the mind is not who we are. You could think of your mind as a computer, a processor of information. Most of us have a computer and we know how much we rely on it. But we also know that a computer sitting on a desk is a separate thing from us. It's not who we are. You wouldn't ask your computer for advice because it doesn't have the wisdom to answer your questions . . . and neither does your mind.

In *A Pilgrim on Tinker Creek*, Annie Dillard says, "The mind is . . . a ceaseless flow of trivia and trash." We think that our thoughts are true; we think we are our thoughts and that we are who we think we are. But, our thoughts are just thoughts . . . and although a few of them are closer to the truth than others, many are opinions, judgments and fantasies. We are not our thoughts. We are not this river of trash and trivia. We ought not swim in the river of our thoughts, much less believe that we are the river. We are more than our thoughts.

We're also not meant to hold on to all of the thoughts and fantasies we have in a day, any more than we would want to collect every piece of junk that floats down a river. A practice of meditation or contemplation helps us rise above the white noise of mental chatter. Sitting in the light of higher consciousness, we watch our thoughts from the bank of the river, waiting for the occasional pearl of insight or treasure chest of inspiration to float by. We pluck from the river that which serves us and we integrate it into our internal repository of knowledge. The rest, the trash and trivia, passes by our view and floats out of sight.

With practice and inner guidance we are better able to discriminate between the ideas that serve us and the thoughts that we don't need to "entertain." With practice, we can decide which thoughts we want to hang out with. Insights come into our mental data bank and integrate into our spiritual wisdom-essence. Knowledge, which is of the mind, increases . . . and wisdom, which is of the Spirit, expands.

In terms of reclaiming lost mental energy, however, learning to quiet our thoughts is one of the most powerful ways we have to manage the personal utility of the mind.

Let's look a little more closely at the structure of thoughts.

First, we have a thought. It may be a conscious thought, or a reactionary thought coming out of our unconscious mind, which has a full file cabinet of past experiences on which we base our core beliefs. The thought or belief is ready and waiting to trigger a reaction to inner or outer stimuli.

So we have a thought that provokes an emotion. The emotion leads us to another thought and another emotional response, which will be an expansion or validation of the previous emotion. We are getting happier, or sadder, or angrier with each thought and resultant emotion.

Spiritual teacher Adyashanti, in his book *The End of Your World*, suggests that when you are in a heightened emotional state, it is helpful to retrace your emotions back to the thought that preceded it, and to the emotion that preceded that thought and so on, until you reach the original thought that started this cascade of thoughts and emotions. Once that original thought is discovered, you can look at what core belief lies beneath that thought. Therein lays the source of the depletion.

Print 120: Some White Lines Indicate Depleting Mental Activity

Whatever the initial depleting thought is, it is an illusion, as the Truth with a capital T does not deplete us. The Truth restores us to our natural completeness. When you are looking at a lip print and you see lines of missing color, (Print 120) these will generally represent depleting thoughts.

LIPSTORY | 158

Print 121: Energized Mental Lines

A depleting thought will lead to a depleting emotion, which will then result in a physical loss of vitality. This is not revelatory information. We all know that our emotional traumas leave us feeling lackluster. What is new is that we can actually see this loss of energy in our lip prints.

If you see energized dark lines, (Print 121) they represent thoughts that are energizing, exciting or overexciting the person. Once again, in general, lines are thoughts and are powered by the mental energetic body.

Let's look at some of these lines.

MENTAL MEMOS

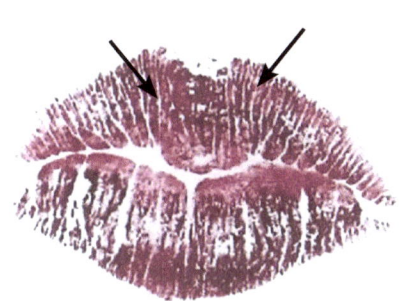

Print 122: Mental Memos

Print 123: Mental Memos

Just as in Prints 122 and 123, Mental Memos are lines that inhabit the upper lip. Like guppies swimming in a fish tank, they have boundaries. For a guppy that would be the glass walls of the aquarium. For Mental Memos, it's the boundaries of the lip outline. They do not cut through the edge of the lip, but are always contained by it. Notice whether the lines are straight, suggesting linear, logical and literal thinking, or branched or squiggly, suggesting creative and/or convoluted thinking. Sometimes they will have little dots on the ends. In this example and the following ones, you will see lines that enter at the top of the upper lip and lines that exit the bottom of the upper lip. Those are not Mental Memos . . . they will be discussed later.

Jilly Eddy calls these internal lines Gerbil Wheels, implying that the mind is like a hamster or a gerbil, running fast and getting nowhere. That's another good analogy. These busy little lines do indicate mental distractions.

Imagine that you have a mental secretary who helps you keep track of the things you say to yourself, especially those things that require action. She sits at her desk in her office in your head and every time you tell yourself something that needs doing, she makes a note on her memo pad. She'll stand by to remind you about it until you actually do the thing or tell her you're not going to do the thing. Each mental memo has a byte of energy attached to it and you don't get that byte of energy back until you have followed through on what you said you would do or you resolve not to do it. The problem is that we forget many of the things we have said to ourselves and these bits of mental energetic "bytes" can accumulate until we begin to have trouble focusing on the present.

The best way to reclaim this trapped energy is to do a Brain Dump. Take some time, over a couple of days to empty your mind of everything you can think of that has any kind of "to do" attached to it. Make a list. A good Brain Dump can fill a couple of pages in a spiral notebook. It's better to write your list, or print it out if you are doing it on a computer, rather than type it on a computer screen or iPad. You want to bring these thoughts into the 3rd dimensional plane. You may be thinking, "I make lists every day," but it's not enough to make a list. You don't get that memo and its energy back from your secretary until you follow through. Also, there are lots of little things that we think and say to ourselves all day long that aren't considered important enough to include in our daily list. Maybe you're driving somewhere and you hear on the radio about a book that you'd like to read, and you think, "I want to buy that book." If you haven't, there is a mental memo in your head. Or maybe you're taking a shower and you think, "I want to try that shampoo my sister uses," but you haven't tried it yet . . . there's a mental memo for that.

Empty your to-dos onto paper for a couple of days, letting old, submerged comments and thoughts surface. Once you feel that you have it all, you must follow-through. Much of what you have written down can be crossed off of the list. You're just not going to dust your baseboards, even if it did seem like a good idea when you thought of it. That recipe you wanted for last Thanksgiving isn't a priority anymore. Cross it off.

Next, do the things on your list, defer them for a later date, or delegate them to someone else. If you defer a task, follow-up and do it by the date you agreed to do so. If you delegate a task to another, be clear about what you expect the other person to do and then follow-up and confirm the task was properly done in the way that you instructed. Your mental secretary, meanwhile, is shredding all of the memos that you have attended to and looking forward to having a clean desk. Remember that making a list is only a first step. You don't get your attention back until you follow through and complete the things on the list!

MENTAL MEMOS IN THE HUG PUCKER

Print 124: Mental Memos in the Hug Pucker

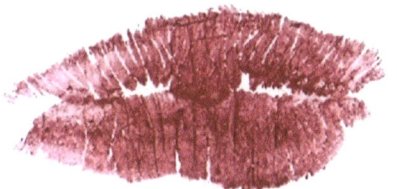

Print 125: Clear Hug Pucker

Memos in the Hug Pucker can indicate thoughts that are distracting the subject in her relationships, causing a loss of or an interference with honest communications. I read a woman one day who had a swarm of lines inside of her Hug Pucker. She confided in me that she had recently reconnected with an old boyfriend. Since she was married, this created a great deal of distraction!

An old boyfriend is one way to be distracted from your closest relationships. You might also be distracted by work, your children's needs, an addictive pattern, a needy parent, or a demanding business partner . . . the possibilities are numerous. When we see lines in the Hug Pucker there is something that is fundamentally distracting the subject from feeling engaged with someone she is close to. Attention to those distractions will be the first step in finding reconnection or resolution.

Notice that the print in Print 125 has no Mental Memos in the Hug Pucker. This print belongs to a very successful author who travels worldwide. She has plenty of things to attend to but her distractions are more "out there" to-dos and tasks rather than things that concern her relationships.

Whatever the source of the distraction, it will cost you energy and focus until you write down and attend to all of the lists and tasks rattling around your head!

WHITE NOISE

Sometimes we see so many lines in the upper lip that they cannot possibly all be Mental Memos. When the upper lip is completely filled with these lines, we have an uber-active mind. This can be seen in the lip prints of bright, busy, responsible people, or people who are discernibly scattered and unfocused. It indicates extreme identification with the mind and thoughts.

Print 126: White Noise

In Print 126 we meet a person with an interstate highway road map in her upper lip! She is immersed in what she thinks and who she thinks she is in the world. She is also a master at multitasking and an over achiever. However, this much mental activity creates a lot of inner noise. It would be a good thing for her to take a few minutes every day to sit in silence, to quiet her mind and allow herself time to dis-identify with her thoughts and activities.

Print 127: White Noise

As we step out of the current of our busy-ness and "doing" we become the witness to our thoughts, and to the thinker of those thoughts. We are less at the effect of them. Thoughts are things and it is our attachment to things that interferes with our inherent peaceful nature. As we become the witness to our thoughts we create a certain distance from them, allowing us to disengage with the thinker and to begin to know ourselves as something more.

Print 127 is a great example of a thought system on hyper drive. The electrical looking lines that are shooting through this print demonstrate a mind on fire with speed-of-light thoughts ricocheting through his consciousness until there's no room for anything but mental activity. The print belongs to a creative and very funny man. He is charismatic, attractive and smart. In his lip print we see a kind of frenetic need to be going and doing . . . but "being" will be difficult inside of a mental freeway like this one. It will be difficult to relax and to connect to others, oneself, and to the present moment in a truly intimate way.

A chaotic tangle of lines in the upper lip sends the message that it's time to take back the asylum from the noisy inmates we call our thoughts! It is a call to develop a practice for quieting the mind. Once again, meditation, prayer, chanting and yoga are all ways to open the doorway to higher consciousness. For those who have trouble sitting still, exercise can help. There are thousands of resources and possible teachers one can turn to for learning how to access your inner silence. Whatever practice suits you, the most important thing is to show up for practice! Your reward for doing so will be an enhanced ability to see through the frenzied illusions of the world and your experience of it. Greater alignment with your true nature is your reward. It is in the silence that you will find your answers. As Ram Dass said, "The quieter you become, the more you can hear."

STRESS (IS ALWAYS A CHOICE!)

Print 128: Stress Lines

Stressed

Stress is a big subject and something that everyone experiences to some degree. The U.S. Surgeon General says that 80% of non-traumatic deaths are stress related, so it's not something to accept or ignore.

Stress lines begin inside of the upper lip and exit the lower edge of the upper lip. (Print 128) Like rivers emptying into the sea, they represent energy flowing down, out and away from your energetic systems. Stress is nothing if not a waste of energy. We hear the expression "a waste of energy" often enough to have forgotten what it actually means. But the literal meaning applies here: energy wasted, a precious commodity thrown away.

Imagine that you have a large push-button in the middle of your chest. Connected to the button is your "default" response, the most common mental and emotional reaction you have to life around you, your "first responder" when things go "wrong." If you have these white lines, your button would be labeled "Stress." Something happens and you don't like it. It could be something someone says or does, or it could be something that occurs or exists. Even though you can't change it, you wish it were different. So you hit your Stress Button. You begin to feel the tension, judgment and frustration of stress. What begins in the mental body quickly bleeds into the emotional and physical. Unchecked, it will become an obsessive thought that cuts you off from your spiritual connections, your intuition and your creativity.

To be clear, we're talking about the kind of stress that depletes you and that has no productive result. It's the stress you feel about things that you can't change.

It's funny how even when we can't change a thing, we, rather insanely, think that throwing our energy at it will have some effect. It's like spending money and getting nothing in return. As spiritual teacher Adyashanti says, when you are stressing, you are having an argument with reality. It's an argument you will always lose.

MENTAL INDICATORS | 163

Here's the good news. The way you respond to any situation is completely your choice. Although we may unconsciously choose stress, or fear, anxiety, disappointment or any of a number of depleting thoughts and emotions, as soon as we are conscious of the state we are in, we have the ability to choose a different response.

Unless you have a psychological or physiological imbalance, the quality of your connection to the world around you is 100% your responsibility. It's your hand that paints the inner landscape of your life. What kind of picture do you want to paint . . . one of stress, emotional turmoil and mental fatigue, or one of serenity in the midst of the usual chaos the world sends our way?

You can't control the actions, thoughts, emotions or words of others, or the events that happen in the world around you. The good news is that no one else can control your beliefs, thoughts, feelings or actions. Which means others cannot cause you to feel anything, including stress. No one and no thing can "make" you have an inner experience that you don't choose to have.

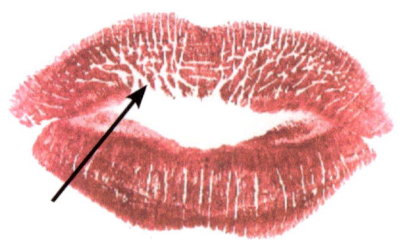

Print 129: Stress Lines

So the first thing to do when you are stressed is to notice that you are! Then own that you are creating the stress yourself. Remember the Stress Button? You have countless other buttons or responses that you could choose. You could look at an event that you feel stressed about and choose to feel compassion or humor, optimism, joy, anticipation or gratitude. Better yet, you could choose neutrality and have no attachment to it being anything other than what it is. Your boss is a jerk? Let him be who he is. You don't have to agree with his behavior. If you can't change him, why spend your precious energy trying to? Step out of your need to have it be otherwise.

If we want more relaxation and harmony internally, we must take ownership of our stress. When you notice yourself stressing, say to yourself . . . the response I'm having is a choice. I am choosing to feel this stress. I can make another choice, or I can keep on stressing. I know that it is costing me energy, focus, productivity, balance, peace, connection to all things and all beings, but I can keep doing it if I choose!

In time you will see the insanity of stressing over things you can't change, and you will begin to choose differently. You'll develop the mental muscles you need to disengage from obsessive thoughts and steer your thoughts in more productive directions.

In Annie Dillard's book *Pilgrim at Tinker Creek*, the author describes watching fish swim into the shade of a tree overhanging the creek. ". . . I see them suspended in a line in deep pools, parallel to the life-giving current, literally 'streamlined.'" Stressing is like turning sideways to the current of life. Learn to streamline. Stop fighting against the rush of reality. Point your nose into the "is-ness" of what life offers you, and allow it to flow around you. Then, when you are rested, swim on.

STRESS IN THE HUG PUCKER

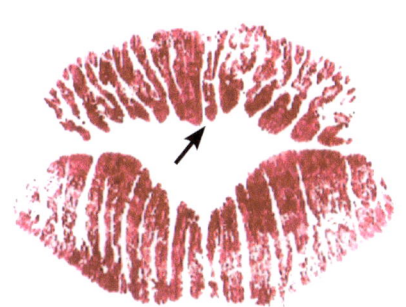

Print 130: Stress in the Hug Pucker

We looked at Mental Memos in the Hug Pucker. Now let's talk about Stress Lines located in the Hug Pucker area. They will refer specifically to stress within a close relationship. It may be stress with a romantic partner, a child, a sibling or another close relative. Even a best friend may show up here. Regaining the energy being lost is still about how you connect the dots between what you perceive "out there" and how you are reacting "in here." Remember that you have choice and can choose not to stress. Take responsibility for your own internal peace.

Be present to the choices you are making as you respond to the actions, behavior and words of others. Being present means not dragging in past grievances or impressions of another and not pulling in fears about the future. It means seeing that situation or person in the present moment without obscuring your view through the filters of what has happened before, or what you are afraid might happen.

If someone is behaving in ways that you find difficult to be with, remember that each of us is on our own journey, and that we each create our own unhappiness and suffering. Have compassion for the other person and look beyond the illusion of anger, fear, blame, or any other form of unawareness you may be stuck in, to the true heart of the person. This is one of the thousand choices you can make other than the "stress" choice. Choose stress and judgment, or choose forgiveness, compassion, humor and relaxation. Stand in the center of peace and speak your truth in beauty. Allow the hand of grace to deliver you back to wholeness and tenderness for the other, and into an understanding of the way forward.

Stressful thoughts close your mind to the true power within you and to the divinity in each of us. When you are feeling stressed and defeated, take a few minutes to breathe in the essence of higher consciousness, allowing yourself to be refreshed. Sit in the light of oneness, streamlining with what is, and relax into the zone of infinite possibilities.

Let me add . . . there is a kind of stress that settles into our bodies, into our muscles and our cells. When we are holding old stress in our bodies, we may want to seek the healing hands of a body worker to help us release the stress that has become embedded in the material body. Body work such as Polarity Balancing, De-Armoring, Shiatsu, Yoga, and deep massage coupled with breath-work can assist us in releasing old stress and reclaiming our inner alignment.

UPPER PEPPERING

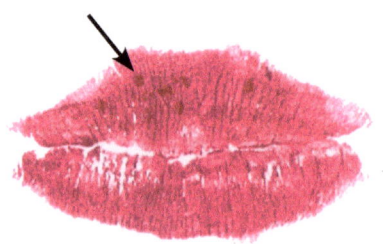

Print 131: Upper Peppering

We saw Peppering in the lower lip earlier as a signal that one is in need of self-care. Peppering in the upper lip is a different kind of signal altogether. These dark specks suggest that the owner of the lips is feeling irritated by someone or something around her. Sometimes there's just one big speck of dark color and sometimes there are a sprinkling of them.

Years ago when I was a student of Native American teachings, our teacher had constructed a large medicine wheel on the floor of our teaching room. We were asked to do an exercise that required each of us to move from one location to another, explaining to our teacher the meaning of each direction and location on the wheel. As I walked with my teacher from the South to the Northwest, I swatted at a gnat that was buzzing around my head. I continued to move to the next direction, but the gnat was all I could think about. After a couple of minutes of this annoying distraction, I finally said, "This bug is driving me crazy!" My teacher stepped in front of me, looked me in the eyes and said. "That bug is taking you out of this ceremony."

And isn't that a great metaphor for what daily irritants do? They take us out of the ceremony of our lives. They distract and anger us, and cause us to lose our perspective, but only if we allow them to. Because, like stress, anger, fear and worry, we have the choice to feel distracted and annoyed, or we can choose to come back into the serenity and sanctuary of the ceremony of our lives.

LINES OF CONCERN

In the upper lip we learned about Mental Memos, White Noise, and Stress. What all of these have in common is that they all involve our thoughts about the "out there," the world around us and how we interface with it.

Print 132: Lines of Concern

In the lower lip we see the mirror image of Mental Memos. Like their "northern" counterparts, these lower white lines begin and end inside the outline of the lip. They also indicate thoughts, but they have to do more with the inner picture than with the world surrounding us "out there." These thoughts have to do with how we relate to ourselves and with our internal goals and failures. Just as those upper lines are a signal that the mind is filled with unattended to action items or an overabundance of random thoughts about life around us, the indications in the lower lip have to do with thoughts about our inner, more private concerns. In fact, we call them Lines of Concern.

If we show depletion in this area, it may be from feeling as though we are not showing up in ways that we would like to, or not doing enough to meet our personal standards. Our uncertainties, doubts and fears, showing as these minor lines inside the lower lip, take us out of the moment. The lines could indicate a need to have more information or to make a plan and set it in place so that we can return to the present.

These are the precursors to full-out regret, distraction and worry, and represent a lack of mindfulness. There is a pattern of allowing the mind to wander, not toward the needs of the outer world, but toward one's personal needs, deficiencies, desires and supposed failings as perceived inside the mind. This is low-level obsessing over past or future events, or a preoccupation with events one imagines may be happening elsewhere.

Print 133: Lines of Concern

When you see these lines in your lip prints, the message is, first, make a list. With the Mental Memos of the upper lip, we asked you to write down all of the actions stored in your mind that you hadn't yet attended to; in essence, a pre-existing list in your head. But with Lines of Concern, you may benefit from coming up with a list of new actions you can take now to build the structure for a desired future. If you worry about your health, make an appointment with a doctor or practitioner now, and go! If you worry because you're overweight, create a wellness plan for yourself, and start moving your body and changing your diet. If you regret not getting your high school diploma, do the research and find out how to get your GED. You may need help and resources. You may need to ask questions and get them answered. The lines in your lips hold a powerful message for you . . . do the things today that will promote the tomorrow you desire so that you can stop worrying about tomorrow and be here now!

Invest time and attention on the actions and attitudes that will take you toward your goals and don't do the things that take you away from them. Be willing to make mistakes. Be consistent, but forgive yourself when you are not. Follow through to completion. Practice gratitude for what you have and where you are on your journey. Begin a practice of meditation or daily prayer. Reach for peace and breathe into the present moment. As self-care and self-love replace self-doubt, presence will naturally override distraction and the present will become the place you most want to be.

WORRY, REGRET AND DISTRACTION

Print 134: Worry, Regret, and Distraction

When the white lines in the lower lip begin to leave the upper edge of the lower lip, we are seeing full-blown worry, distraction and/or regret. Just like the Stress Lines of the upper lip, these lower indicators signal life-force draining out of one's field of vitality. This mental depletion dominos as the emotions come into play with feelings of fear and loss, and the other aspects of energy become involved, as well. Emotions are thoughts we are feeling in our physical body, and so we see physical fatigue, loss of libido and creativity, leading to disconnection from spirit. But it begins with a thought, and thoughts continue to stoke the fire of fear and worry.

Worry

There are at least 2 ways to interact with the future. The first is to set goals and take actions to create structures that will support achieving those goals. You do these things in the present with enthusiasm. You create excitement, anticipation and optimism in the present. You plan for the future without worrying or obsessing about it. You save money, teach your children how to be safe, invest in education, and maintain your health and possessions. You stay present and enjoy your life in the now, allowing the future to unfold moment by moment.

Print 135: Worry Lines

The other way that we can interact with the future is to worry about it. When we worry, instead of building on our goals in the present, we create an imaginary future where bad things happen. We visit that imaginary place often. We spend time there. We pass precious moments of our life in a place that does not exist . . . a hall of illusion. There is no life in this imaginary future. It isn't real. We made it up! But we go there and sit and when we return to the present, we bring our imaginary place with us like a toxic cloud that distorts our vision and our ability to see clearly what's right in front of us. With this fog of fear and worry surrounding us, we are unable to fully connect to the blessings, opportunities and pure potential that are always within and around us.

If you see these lines in your lips, remind yourself that nothing ever happens in the future . . . never, ever. Events always happen in the present moment when we can make choices and take action, when we can choose to stress or to accept.

I often ask my clients, "Do you have anything to worry about right now?" If they say yes, I know that they have just gone somewhere in their mind, away from me and the moment we are sharing. When they say no, it is usually with the realization that when you are present there is almost never anything to worry about. There may be actions to take and choices to make, but worry does not exist when you are completely in the core of the moment. We have to go to an imaginary place to worry.

Worry lines are a strong call for mindfulness, for learning to appreciate and honor the gift of presence. Staying present is one of the hardest things to do as a human. That's why you hear so many gurus, teachers and philosophers teaching about the practice. The Vietnamese Zen Buddhist monk Thich Nhat Hanh teaches the "Art of Mindful Living" in his books. Ram Dass brought the phrase "Be Here Now" into the hippy consciousness in the 1970's. Everyone from Buddha to Yogananda, Depok Chopra, Pema Chodrin, Marianne Williamson, Eckhart Tolle and Oprah Winfrey speak of the importance of staying in an awareness of the present. Today there's even a *Mindfulness for Dummies* book. Mindfulness is being taught in the workplace and as a stress reducer, a problem solving technique and a form of meditation. Mindfulness is the awareness of life. It is connection to oneself and to the unity of all things.

The importance of staying present cannot be overstated. Each moment of life is precious and we will never have another chance to experience it. If we spend our time in an imaginary and scary place, we will miss our lives.

Poet David Wagoner writes:
> Wherever you are is called Here,
> And you must treat it as a powerful stranger,
> Must ask permission to know it and be known.

There are many techniques for coming into the present that are helpful. Buddha described mindfulness this way, "We sit, we walk, we eat. But when we sit, we know we are sitting, when we walk, we know we are walking, when we eat, we know we are eating." In his book, *Living Buddha, Living Christ*, Thich Nhat Hahn says, "When you have mindfulness, you have love and understanding, you see more deeply, and you can heal the wounds in your own mind."

Presence also asks you to let go of the past, or rather, to give up seeing everything and everyone through the filter of the past. One of the meditations in *A Course in Miracles* is "I see only the past." One interpretation of that is that when we look at someone, we see him through the muddy window of our past experience with that person. How different our relationships would be, especially the difficult ones, if we were willing to meet others each time with an open and unimpeded heart, rather than dragging our past grievances into the circle of our encounters.

Meditation and breath-work are good ways to get present. Connecting to your inner energetic body and feeling the glow and radiance of it flowing through your hands, feet, legs, arms, torso and head, will get you into the moment. The practice, the hard part, is staying in the present moment. When you remember what is at stake, it is worth the effort.

Regret

White lines in the lower lip can also represent regret. I can't tell by looking whether the lines show regret or worry. Sometimes I ask, and sometimes I just address both, as it is often a combination of the two that the lines are indicating.

When we are lost in regret over a past event, we are traveling out of the moment into another imaginary time and place. Memory is a construct of the mind. Only the now really exists, but the past we imagine moves into the present, claiming its territory, when we keep it alive in our minds and thoughts. We tell ourselves the story of what happened. We describe the past to ourselves and to others in a way that makes us feel

Print 136: Regret Lines

regret about what happened. But we are actually fixating on what we believe to be the meaning of what happened and not on what actually happened.

Let me remind you of the old parable about the three blind men who were asked to describe an elephant. The one touching the truck thought that an elephant was like a large snake. The one touching a leg thought the elephant was like a tree, and the one holding the tail thought that an elephant was a rope. Not one of them had the complete picture. None of them had all of the information needed to accurately describe what an elephant looked like. In the same way, events happen and there are the facts about what happened, but we remember any event based on our point of view at the time. We do well to remember that we didn't and still don't have all of the facts about what happened. If we had different information, we might see it differently. There might be a new way of seeing the past that would actually change one's perception and create room for healing.

If we have attachment to a past event and feel regret that it didn't happen the way we wish it had, then we are layering our painful perceptions onto a tiny corner of what actually happened. It's like picking up one piece of a large jigsaw puzzle, and thinking you see the whole picture. The pain of regret that we feel is in the story we are telling ourselves about what happened, but we don't and really can never know all of the dynamics, the purpose and higher meaning of past experiences. Everything that happens, every challenge we are presented with is meant to help us expand our awareness and come into alignment with our divine nature. If we are dwelling on something from the past, we have not yet understood the teaching that is still being offered to us through the experience, and therefore it is still taking our attention and energy out of the present moment. This will show in our lip prints as missing energy and color.

As we begin to appreciate the value of our painful memories, we can begin, at last, to harvest the wealth of understanding that lies buried in each one. Like acorns waiting to take root, each distressing memory is a gift of unrealized potential. Be willing to sit with the pain and with the story. Ask for clarity. Be grateful for what happened, even before you know exactly what will be revealed to you. Surrender to the gift being offered. The pain you feel is in your mind. The wisdom and peace that lie within the experience will, when you are ready, come through your heart.

Distraction

Print 137: Lines of Distraction

The third possibility, when we see these lines in the lower lip, is that the subject doesn't stay present because she allows her mind to leave her present location with preoccupations. Maybe she is wondering how her child did on a test at school, or concerned that her husband hasn't called. Her friend is having medical tests done and she is mentally at the hospital with her. It doesn't have to be full-blown worry or regret that takes her away, but the end result is a departure from the moment, right here, right now, where life begins and ends. The result is much the same whether you are worried, regretful or projecting yourself elsewhere. The world is spinning, life is happening and you have left it to go somewhere in your head.

By all means, use your mind to plan the logistics of your life, but strive to be present. Live your life, with all of its pleasures and possibilities, in the present moment. Our lips, like so many revered spiritual teachers, remind us to be mindful and not mind-full.

GALE MARKS

A Gale Mark is a white line that cuts completely through the upper or lower lip. Jilly Eddy named this indicator after a friend whose name was Gayle. Finding the meaning of the Gale Mark was a bit of serendipity that affirms for me how Divine Consciousness will step in sometimes and give us a hint (Gayle's name) to help us understand the mysterious.

Jilly's friend had this mark cutting through her lip prints and Jilly wanted to figure out its meaning. It happened that Gayle was going through a very difficult time in her life. Jilly began seeing this mark in other people who were having a tough time. The death of a loved one, divorce, loss of home, a feeling of separation . . . any one of these events can feel like a gale storm blowing through our lives and leveling the landscape. In time, Jilly confirmed that this mark represents great challenges either in the present or in the past, usually, but not always, associated with the loss of or separation from someone close.

When we see a Gale Mark in the upper lip, the person having a difficult time is sharing his or her challenges with others, or the difficulty still presently involves others. So someone might be in a tough custody battle with an ex-spouse, and the Gale Mark would be in the upper lip. Or someone may have lost a loved one, but feels a need to rely on and seek counsel from others. The upper lip Gale Mark shows that the subject is reaching out and talking about the problem with others.

Print 138: Upper Gale Mark

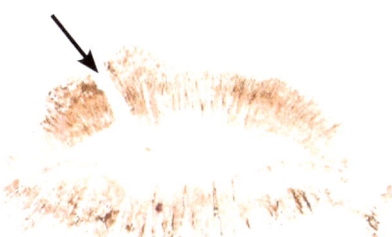

Print 139: Gale Mark

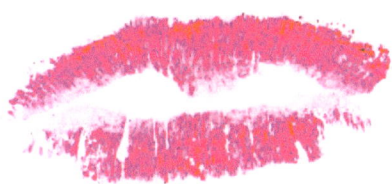

Print 140: No Gale Mark

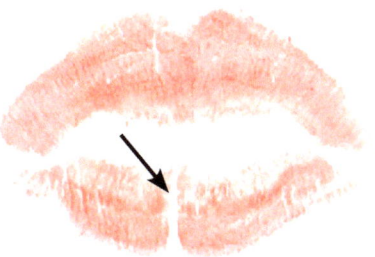

Print 141: Lower Gale Mark

In Print 138, the person was getting a divorce. His wife was trying to take possession of the house that he owned, and he was in a legal battle with her. His home meant a great deal to him and the prospect of losing it and the life he had hoped for with his wife were devastating him. He was eager to talk about it to his friends and was processing his grief (and anger) by verbalizing his feelings.

Prints 139 and 140 belong to a friend of mine who lost his daughter and son-in-law in a car accident several years ago. I took the first print, 139, shortly after the accident. At the time he was also facing challenges in his relationship with his adult son. Both situations required him to manage some legalities, so there were other people involved by necessity. There's no doubt he had every reason to have a Gale Mark in his lip print. Print 140 was taken a couple of years later after he and his son had healed their relationship and he had had time to accept the loss of his daughter. As you can see, the Gale Mark is gone.

If the mark is only in the lower lip, as in Print 141, the subject is holding the pain inside and not discussing it much with others. It could be an old pain, like the early loss of a parent that has never been fully accepted. It could be a present situation, but still the person would be dealing with it alone.

If there are Gale Marks in both lips (Print 142), there is inner holding and an outer expression or experience happening simultaneously. This print belongs to a gentleman I met one night at an event. In the course of the reading, I asked him about some past experience that still troubled him. He opened up immediately and told me that he had served some years in prison for drug offenses.

MENTAL INDICATORS | 173

Print 142: Gale Marks
Upper and Lower

When I spoke to him about his ability to mentor and to be an image-maker for others, he got tears in his eyes and couldn't speak for a moment. Then he showed me his AA bracelet and told me how he had been mentoring kids and that his deepest desire was to be of service. We talked about the need for him to stay open to receiving the lessons of those years without dwelling on the past . . . without seeing himself through the filter of his past mistakes.

A Gale Mark is an amplification of Regret, and the pathway to relief is similar. The energy that is being directed towards the experience, and lost to the subject, will continue to leak away until the owner of the lips is willing to open to the lesson inherent in the cause of the Gale Mark.

Once again, we are called to understand that each difficult time in our lives is a gift from a benevolent universe. Until we open to what the experience is trying to teach us, we will be stuck with the pain and inner turmoil, stuck with bitterness, anger and grief. The presence of a Gale Mark means that one has not fully understood and received the full measure of the teaching in the experience. We haven't yet completely unwrapped the gift. We must remain receptive to the lesson being offered until we feel the relief of realignment. Our mind will not take us there. This is the work of Spirit and Grace. We ask for wisdom and wait with an open heart until we reawaken to our connection to all things and to everyone. As we soften into forgiveness, the energy will return to us, the Gale Marks will close, and we will be restored to balance and peace. Once again, our challenges, when embraced and explored, are always about our own evolution.

WORRY AND GALE MARKS IN THE GLS

When we see a deep line of missing color in the cleft of the Gourmet Lip Split (Print 143), we can legitimately discuss with the subject all of the wonderful qualities of the GLS. But we can also observe that there is a level of worry about one's ability to provide for oneself or to satisfy one's appetites. So this can refer to the state of someone's physical love life, to one's unmet desires or to the state of one's bank account.

Look at the depth of the split and you'll get an idea of how deep the level of concern is. In the Print 144 a Line of Worry has become a Gale Mark.

Print 143: Worry Line in the GLS

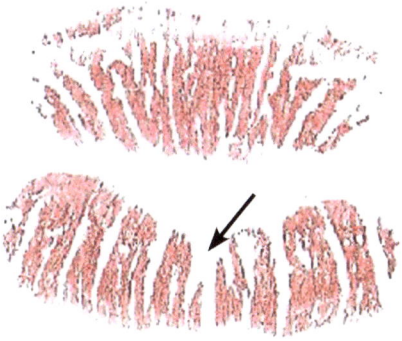

Print 144: Gale Mark in the GLS

Print 145: Gale Mark in the GLS

Print 146: No Gale Mark in the GLS

A Gale Mark in the GLS will indicate a traumatic time that is affecting income and lifestyle. And the load is being borne internally. Again we have two prints from the same person, made at different times. In Print 145, we see that the lower lip has been split in two. The woman who made this print was under financial stress and in danger of losing her home as well as her mother's. At the time, her mother had fallen ill and needed constant care. This young woman was working three jobs and caring for her mother and several pets. Her lip print shows that she was "coming apart at the seams." I knew her when this was all going on and she presented herself as composed and capable of dealing with what must have felt like a crumbling life-structure. To me, her lip print is a profile in courage.

In Print 146 we see her print three years later. By then she was engaged to be married, her mother was doing well. All of the pets were being cared for without stress. While we still see some worry, her Gale Mark had reconnected and she was on her way to feeling whole again.

MENTAL INDICATORS | 175

EMOTIONAL INDICATORS

EMOTIONAL MOTTLING

In general, emotional indicators show up as fading in a lip print. Thoughts are lines and feelings show as faded areas.

Print 147: Emotional Mottling

We have previously seen mottling or splotchy, spotty color discussed as a physical indicator, but as mentioned, it can also be an indicator of chronic low-grade emotional depletion. This makes sense when we understand that emotions are thoughts converted to feelings, and feelings can be both emotional and physical in their expressions.

On occasion, mottling may indicate that addictive patterns are involved as a way of dulling the discomfort of the emotional imbalance. I recently read the prints of a young man who appeared to be in excellent physical shape, and yet he had mottled lip prints. He confided that he was a recovering heroin addict. Alcohol abuse, poor eating habits, smoking, lack of proper sleep and exercise can all contribute to mottling. These physical manifestations are a symptom of the core issue, which, again, will be emotion based. There may be an internalization of feelings of loss, betrayal, helplessness and feeling like a victim. There may be self-esteem issues. Mottling suggests a need to redirect the thoughts and activities in healthier and more self-affirming directions.

Print 148: Mottled Energy

Even if the source of the mottling is emotional, physical self-care will help raise self-esteem and energy levels in all aspects.

As you learn to interpret the specific meaning of fading in each area of a lip print, remember to present each message in a positive, hopeful and affirming manner. This can be done with authenticity only when you are present to the gifts inherent in each indicator. There are no "bad" indicators. There are only helpful messages intended to assist us in our journey toward health and greater awareness.

CHALLENGE LINE

Challenge Lines

An emotional indicator that you will see often is the Challenge Line. It appears as a band of fading that creates an arc across the upper lip. Sometimes it spans the entire lip, and sometimes it is broken into pieces. It may stretch across the middle, the upper or the lower third of the lip and there may be more than one line in a lip. If the fading passes through the Hug Pucker area, it may pertain to a close relationship.

My general sense of the location of the Challenge Line is that the farther up from the Hug Pucker the line is, the more it moves out of the inner circle into the realm of work and world.

Usually the fading will become more exaggerated with each additional print. Sometimes the first lip print will seem to be solid and then the second will be completely washed out. Even in these cases, you will usually see a hint of the Challenge Line in the first print. Look at our next example in Print 149. If energy is color, notice how much energy is missing in lip print #2 compared to print #1.

1 **2** **3**

Print 149: Challenged

LIPSTORY | 178

Challenge lines represent energy we are giving away to feelings of disappointment. You may be experiencing some secondary emotion, such as anger, sadness or victimization, but the underlying feeling is one of disappointment. We are either disappointed in the behavior of a person, or in a life situation. It could be something big like the perceived betrayal of a friend or coworker. Maybe we've had a financial loss. Perhaps we have an illness that is difficult to deal with, or our spouse has been unfaithful. Certainly the death of a loved one would show as disappointment. On the other hand, the cause of the fading could be one of life's smaller disappointments, the kind that happen on a daily basis. Someone was rude to you at the grocery store or the cake you ordered isn't what you wanted, or you spilled red wine on your favorite blouse.

Disappointment wears many masks, but when we feel disappointment it's because we think someone should be doing things differently, or that a situation isn't what it is supposed to be. Similar to stress, this is an argument with reality. We are being judgmental about someone or about something, and the failure to have our expectations met is draining us of power. We are out of agreement with the world around us, and just like the color in the print, something is missing. Our clarity and vision have been compromised.

For many of us, challenges come and go, like clouds floating across a blue sky. Others of us have challenges that are persistent, i.e. an ailing family member or persistent poverty. Disappointment may have become an accepted way of life. A person may not even be aware of the chronic feeling of being "let down" by life in general.

Whether the challenge is temporary or long-lasting, it is important to set about recovering the energy that is escaping the luminosity of the person with a Challenge Line. Once again, like the blind man holding the tail of the elephant, we can never see the whole picture, but there are a multitude of ways to perceive any situation. Some will cause us to suffer. Some will bring us peace and offer us previously unimagined solutions. We are wise to seek the latter.

The pathway to restoring balance runs through Divine Consciousness, not through your mind or emotions. You cannot solve a problem on the level of the problem, and your thoughts, judgments and emotions are where the problem began. Trying to think your way out of what you are thinking and feeling is like trying to rearrange the deck chairs on the Titanic. If your mind could deliver a solution to you, you would be at peace by now.

Open your heart and awareness to a new and higher perspective. Whether your beliefs call you to prayer, meditation or contemplation, there is a way of seeing the situation that will restore your harmony. Ask for it. Turn your attention toward whatever form of Benevolent Awareness you believe and trust in, and ask to see the situation differently. You are asking for an act of Grace. Stay open and wait until it comes to you.

In the moment that you receive the gift of a new perception you will be restored, re-empowered and refreshed. The illusions of fear and judgment will disappear and you will come back into alignment with your higher consciousness. Disappointment becomes transformation, and fear retreats in the face of love. What was missing is restored. Forgiveness and compassion return. In fact, you may see that there is nothing that needs forgiving. If that seems impossible to you now, then you have some idea of the miracle that awaits.

Your Challenge Line is asking you to have faith that Divine Consciousness is always working to your benefit and that every disappointment is offered as a teaching that will lead you into greater connection and wisdom.

In the end, it doesn't matter what the actual challenge is when we understand the purpose of challenges in general. We will look more deeply at that purpose as we explore the Journey Line.

JOURNEY LINE

We now know that horizontal fading across the upper lip represents an emotional response of disappointment about someone or something outside of oneself. In the lower lip a similar faded band across the lip represents disappointment in oneself. It indicates critical self-talk, an inner discourse with ourselves that depletes us and defines us mistakenly as less than the integrated, multidimensional sacred human beings that we are. I call this faded band the Journey Line.

Notice in this first example that the left print has a dark background, but is displaying a wide faded area in the lower lip. The second and third prints show major emotional depletion . . . the upper lip is washed out with a Challenge Line and the lower lip has all but disappeared. The owner of the lips has distinct physical power, as evidenced by the dark background of her first print, but her inner power, at the time she made the prints, was diminished by disappointment from within and without (which is still really an experience of "within"). Let us look more closely at this indicator and what it teaches us.

We have all felt the personal disappointment of not living up to our own standards. We've turned on ourselves with that judgmental inner voice, and taken our inner child out behind the woodshed for a whooping. We, better than anyone, know our own failings and flaws and will be the first to pile on the criticism when we make a mistake, or when we fall short somehow. Most of us do this because we have never been given another model for how to have that inner conversation. We learned from our parents, our peers, and our community to punish ourselves when we fail in any way. There is a sense in our culture that it is a high vibrational act to self-flagellate. I disagree.

When we do this, when we turn on ourselves in disappointment and self-loathing, we have forgotten the big picture of our lives.

Think of it this way. One day we are born and one day we will die. In between those two events we live our lives, moving through our days either in a fog of illusion, caught up in the maya of the world, or in conscious awareness. If we are paying attention, we know that we are here to love, to learn and to evolve into an awakened state. Every day we are given opportunities to do so. Each challenge, failure and success offers us the possibility to refine ourselves.

Every time we make a mistake we are being given a gift, and if we are willing to unwrap it and look inside, we will see something that is of benefit to us. You know from your own experience that you are a better person today because of mistakes you have made in the past. You might even be willing to say that you are grateful for something that you really suffered through. We learn from our mistakes and failures, and we mature. This is the journey that we are on. It is a sacred journey of moving into awareness. We walk the road, stepping beyond fear and illusion into wisdom, compassion, peace and love. Our ongoing evolution is the primary purpose of our existence.

The possibility of becoming the most enlightened, awake and aware expression of yourself is the gift that you are being offered in each moment and with every challenge. This is the direction your mistakes and all the bits and pieces of yourself with which you find fault are taking you, toward reintegrating those pieces into a greater whole. Every time you break through self-condemnation and emerge into the light of self-love and acceptance, you move a step closer to greater refinement. When you accept the gift of each challenge, you clear the way for expansion into realization and divine alignment. Self-love and self-appreciation are not selfish concepts on the level of Spirit. Learning to love the Divine within yourself and to appreciate Its' presence and purpose in the process of your life will bring you out of the distortion of self-judgment into peace, gratitude, and a life of purpose.

I know that your mother taught you to say thank you when you receive a gift. Even if you don't know what's in it and even when you don't like the wrapping, you can still say thank you with sincerity and with a sense of anticipation. All day long the universe is hand delivering one gift after another to your doorstep, every one of them intended to lead you out of illusion into enlightenment. Can you find a feeling of gratitude in your heart for the Benevolence that continuously blesses you? Can you begin to have faith that even when you don't like the wrapping a gift comes in, it is still a gift worth receiving, and deserving of gratitude?

Everything is a gift. The Challenge Line represents a gift. Stress lines, Mental Memos, worry and regret are all gifts designed to open your heart to universal abundance and love.

And speaking of gifts and giving, we can't give what we don't have. If we don't know how to give ourselves approval and appreciation, how can we not feel disappointed, as well, by others? This is why you'll so often see a Journey Line coupled with a Challenge Line.

Self-judgment is an enormous drain of energy and luminosity. You can literally feel the energy drain from you when you realize that you have made a mistake. Begin to notice the voice in your head and when you hear the judgment and the emotional flaying begin, just stop. Say to yourself, "I don't know why I should be grateful for this thing that I am unhappy about, but right now I am going to say thank you until I understand its purpose. There is a teaching here for me, and I have complete faith in the sacred process of my life. I will wait with anticipation and gratitude for the beauty of this experience to be revealed to me."

Don't wait days, weeks or years after a mistake to recover or to experience self-love and forgiveness. This practice of gratitude will teach you to regain your peace sooner. In time, you may learn to recover in seconds from what you might have spent days obsessing over in the past. Turning the inner voice into a voice of gratitude is a more energizing conversation to have than the depleting voice of self-judgment. You begin, with practice, to recapture the energy that has been leaking out of you for most of your life. With gratitude, you become present to the bigger picture of how the curriculum of your life is presented to you. And as you bless each disappointment and failure with a heart-felt "thank you", you honor the sacred journey of your life.

FADED APEX

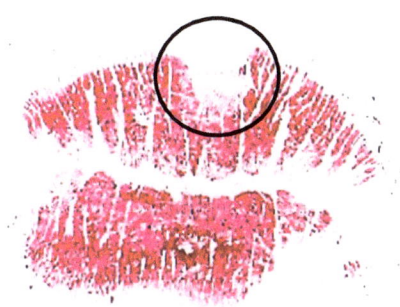

Print 150: Faded Cupid's Bow

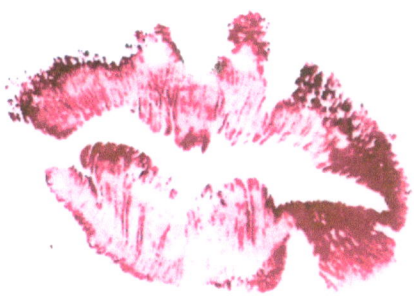

Print 151: Faded Apex and People Movers

Print 152: Faded Apex on a Smooth Top

Now and then you'll see that a person has fading in the area of the Cupid's Bow, or the apex of the lips. If the fading is extensive, it may be difficult to make out whether or not there even is a Cupid's Bow.

Remember that the apex of the lip, where we would find the Cupid's Bow, is where we see a person's desire to find balance and harmony with others. The person with a Cupid's Bow is the negotiator, the seeker of the win-win solution. Why does she seek this balance? Perhaps it is because she has firmly held beliefs about fairness and equanimity, but the owner of the Cupid's Bow also cares about the opinions of others, and in some respects, she fears their judgment.

So if she were concerned that others didn't hold a high enough opinion of her, or that they didn't appreciate her for who she is and what she offers, and if she valued the opinion of these others, then we would expect her to feel some loss of energy that would result in fading in the lip print. The Cupid's Bow is where that fading occurs.

At times we'll see fading in the points extending up above the lip line called People Movers. (Print 151) This suggests that even as the person is extending self-expression and her opinions out to the people around her, as she is leading others, she is feeling doubt about her leadership and about being supported. When the area between the People Movers is faded, there is an additional sense of not being appreciated.

What about Smooth-Tops? It can be difficult to distinguish between a highly positioned Challenge Line and a Faded Apex, especially in a Smooth-Top. But even though they are a little less concerned with the opinions of others, Smooth-Tops may still respond to a perceived lack of appreciation with fading in the apex. (Print 152)

How do we retrieve the missing energy that leaves us when we don't feel appreciated?

The spiritual teacher Eckhart Tolle talks about the roles we take on in his book *A New Earth*. He explains that the problem is not that we take on roles, the role of mother, the role of teacher, the role of caretaker . . . but that we believe that we are the role we are playing . . . we become attached to and we identify with the role of mother or teacher or wife or corporate leader or committee chairperson or nurse.

Perhaps we have cast ourselves as a victim, as helpless, as a conspiracy theorist or a maverick. By definition a role is something we "play," a psychological costume that we consciously or unconsciously slip into in certain of our life arenas. We can do great good and participate in a grand vision of life when we are aware of the role we are being called on to take. However, a vast majority of people wear their roles unconsciously and have lost touch with the unchanging, eternal self that has donned the uniform of a specific expression and lifestyle. When we submerge ourselves in a role (what Eckhart Tolle calls the "form") and then we lose the role because the need for it is taken away, we are left groundless with no idea of who we are and how we should relate to the world around us.

Think of the mother whose children leave home, the long-time caretaker whose patient dies, the professional athlete who retires, or the army vet who comes home from war. Any one of these people may feel lost once the object of their identification is removed. It is the identification with and the attachment to the roles we play that create suffering for us. Often the roles we play make us feel empowered and good about ourselves. Other times we play disempowering roles, for example, that of victim or one who has been betrayed, but oddly we find power in the strength of our identification with disempowerment. We may identify with the role of Loser, Addict, Prostitute, or Rebel, and we are empowered by the belief that we know who we are. Whether our role makes us appear good or bad, if we think that we are any of these identities, we have forgotten who we really are. We will either be unable to move out of that identity or we will feel grief, disorientation, despair, and reluctance when we are forced to.

Print 153: Faded Cupid's Bow

How does this relate to the faded Cupid's Bow? The person with the fading has adopted a false reality. She believes her "role" is not being appreciated by others. In her disappointment she has taken on the role of victim or martyr. Her perception is that others do not understand her value, which in and of itself is no cause for depletion. She could make her observation from a place of neutrality or curiosity. "Oh, look, they don't seem to be aware of the purpose and beauty with which I lead my life. Isn't that interesting?" Instead she has made appreciation from others a "should." "They 'should' appreciate me!" If she feels wounded, it is because she is attached to being perceived in a certain way, and therefore feels like a victim on some level because that isn't happening. Her identity has become the misunderstood victim, or even the martyr.

It may be true that she is surrounded by people who don't appreciate who she is and what she contributes, but that has no power to defeat her unless she has forgotten who she is. When she forgets who she is, she may begin to believe that she does not deserve to be appreciated. When she is in alignment with a sense of her worth as a Sacred Human Being, she can observe the reactions of others without being attached to them. This is not the same as the ego saying, "I don't care what you think." This is being conscious of and present to the sacred in everyone. Attachment to the opinions of others brings pain. Connection to the heart of others brings peace.

It is enough to simply say to someone with a faded apex: Remember who you are. You are a Sacred Child of God, and you are perfect. If others do not see or appreciate that, it doesn't become any less true. Stand in alignment with your spiritual beauty and allow the radiance of your being to extend outward to those around you. They are on their own journey of awakening and you are on yours. Your job is to love yourself and to love them, in the face of any illusions of lovelessness. As *A Course in Miracles* says . . . only the love is real.

COMMUNICATION GAP

We know that missing color means missing energy and some sort of depletion. And we know that the Hug Pucker is where we look to see clues regarding how someone is feeling about or communicating with those he is closest to.

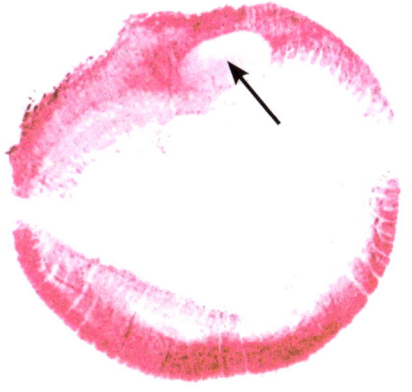

Print 154: Communication Gap

So if there is missing color or fading in the Hug Pucker, we may deduce that something is amiss. When color is missing in the Hug Pucker, we call it a Communication Gap, as it represents a breakdown in communication between the subject and someone close to or important to the subject.

Here is a good example of a Communication Gap. (Print 154) It belongs to a gentleman who used to work for one of the local TV stations in Phoenix, Arizona. He interviewed me for an early morning segment on Valentine's Day several years ago. He wanted to give me his lip prints on camera, so when the segment began and the camera went live, he put on some lipstick with a comical flourish. From the audio feed back in the studio, I could hear the old instrumental song "The Stripper" being played as he applied the color. When he handed me his lip print, I was so surprised by the size of his Communication Gap, that I was almost speechless.

Since he had begun the interview with the campy playfulness of a large man putting on lipstick, we continued the interview in a playful way and I kept his reading general and fun. Later I sent a full reading of what I had seen in his print to his address at the TV station. I never heard back from him, and I learned soon afterwards that he had left the TV station and had moved to California. Whatever the reason for his move to California, on that particular morning, he was experiencing a breakdown in communication between himself and someone important to him.

Print 155: Same Subject without Communication Gap

I saw this same gentleman recently when he was back in town for a performance. He still works in California at a TV station there, and is pursuing a career in music. His latest lip print (Print 155) suggests that he is feeling much more connected to those around him than he was on that morning five years ago.

When we don't trust others enough to be completely honest, or when we are fearful of speaking our truth, others get it on some level. Holding back your truth creates disconnection and a loss of intimacy. If you have a Communication Gap, there is someone in your life with whom you are not sharing your honest feelings, and from whom you are, therefore, experiencing some separation.

People with Zingers will tell me that they don't have any trouble speaking their mind. That's true. But I'm talking about speaking your heart, not your mind. "Zinger-speak" is communication with an agenda, which is fine in appropriate situations. But the kind of depletion we see in a Communication Gap is caused when we are afraid that if we say what's really in our heart to someone whose opinion matters to us, it could be risky.

Native American teachings have much to say about heart-felt communication. They explain that water and plants can teach us how to articulate our innermost truth "in a Beauty Way." Water teaches us to allow our truth to flow unimpeded, without damming it up. It takes energy to hold back what wants to be expressed and that spent energy shows as the missing color in the Hug Pucker. Dams can break, however, and when they do, the result is usually destructive. Alternatively, dammed up water can become

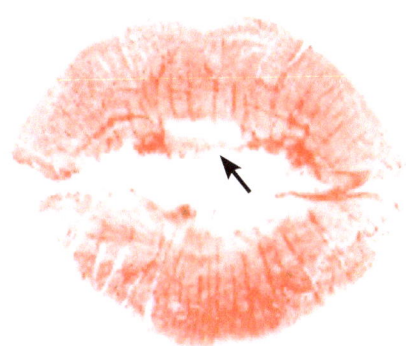

Print 156: Communication Gap

stagnant, breeding pestilence. Holding back water or your truth can lead to negative consequences, ironically the very thing you are trying to avoid! Better to surrender to emotional fluidity. Just like a woodland brook, your truth, when spoken with beauty, will nurture life around you.

Plants also have their place in this conversation. Think of how much plants give to us and in how many ways. Plants feed us and give us the materials to build shelter. They provide clean air, clothing, fuel, and a thousand conveniences that we hardly notice from books to wine to life-saving medicines. Yet they give themselves to us unconditionally, with no expectation of reward or even gratitude. Imagine picking a lemon off of a tree. The lemon tree doesn't say, "What are you going to do with that?" It just says, "Lemon," and lets it go.

We learn from plants to give our truth in the same way, with no conditions, expectations or attachments. When you feel hesitant to say what is in your heart and are afraid that you won't say it right or that you'll be judged or misunderstood, think to yourself, "How can I say this in a Beauty Way?" Speaking in Beauty is simply saying, "What's true for me is this . . ." and then you yield to the natural unfolding and expression of your thoughts without any agenda, and with no attachment or manipulation. You speak, not to coerce or pressure another, not to gain favor, not to change anything or to make it stay the same. You speak to free yourself, and in that moment, you free everyone around you.

When we practice this form of communication, our relationships become more authentic, trust deepens and we are empowered by the very act of standing in our own truth. The intimacy that you desire comes more easily. You will ultimately find your way to greater emotional mastery.

You don't always have to speak when you feel hesitant. But if you don't, you must own the cost of silence. It costs you vitality, connection, intimacy, and the integrity that comes with being honest. So make it a practice, and when you cannot do it, be patient with yourself. You'll have another opportunity.

On a practical note, if you are in an unsafe situation, do what you must to be safe, but unless you are living with someone who is violent, or you are in a situation where your physical well-being is threatened, then take this on as a daily practice. Practice emotional fluidity. Speak your truth in tenderness and in beauty . . . and let it go. Be a lemon tree.

TIPSY LIP PRINTS

This indicator combines mottling with position. One or more of the lip prints are at an angle. Tipsy Lip Prints, or Topsy-Turvy Lip Prints as Jilly Eddy calls them, resemble leaves blowing in the wind. The person making the prints may be feeling at the mercy of the winds of life.

Combined with extreme mottling, Tipsy Lips mean that the person is feeling off balance. There may be a sense of chaos and disorder, of uncertainty or helplessness.

In this example (Print 157) we see a lip print on the left that is standing on its axis and, on the right, tipping upward toward the future. There is a sense that the person is hoping to move away from a past that threw her off her center towards a future about which she is hopeful and yet a bit fearful.

Print 157: Tipsy Lip Prints

This young woman had just gotten out of prison and was about to enter rehab.

Tipsy Lips are an indication of a kind of emotional free-fall. There is a need to ground one's self, to find something to anchor to during a time of some degree of chaos. During these times the best thing to do is to learn to surf the chaos and not fall off the board! Occasional periods of uncertainty give us the opportunity to redefine ourselves and to integrate the wisdom that we have learned in the recent past. It's a good time to discard old patterns and beliefs that no longer serve us, and to determine anew where we want to stand in the world.

LINE OF OVERWHELM

Upper Only   Lower Only   Upper and Lower

Lines of Overwhelm

When we are feeling overloaded with too much to do, we experience it as a heightened mental/emotional state in combination with a physically depleted condition. The degree of our feeling of overwhelm may range from a mild sense of feeling slightly stretched out of our comfort zone, and needing to juggle lots of tasks, all the way to a deep sense of urgency and fearing that we are losing ground. The intensity of the emotion shows in a lip print as a dark line on the outer edge of the upper and/or lower lip print. If the person has the outline on the upper lip, she is sharing her feelings with others. If she only has the line on her lower lip, she is suffering and coping in silence and others may not be aware of how full her plate is or that she could use some help. If the line is present on both lips, she is asking for help, but not feeling as though she is getting enough.

Notice in our examples that the outline is often coupled with a Challenge Line or a Journey Line. By its very nature, this indicator wouldn't show without the contrast of the missing color of one of these faded bands. So we have emotional intensity along with disappointment in oneself or another. This is not a recipe for success!

The dark outer line resembles a boundary of sorts, and this is the message of a Line of Overwhelm. A person with this indicator is being asked to learn to set boundaries. She has allowed work, her daily tasks, other people or life to submerge her in more than she can handle. She may be a people pleaser who just can't say "no" when someone asks her to do something. Or perhaps she has ambitions that drive her to reach beyond her present capability to manage things. It could be that her employer is asking too much of her, and she is disappointed in herself and in him. Or, she may be completely competent and capable of doing what is being asked of her, but she doesn't believe that she is and so she feels the frustration and desperation of it all being too much!

There can be a lot of misplaced and lost energy in the experience of overwhelm. The first thing to do when you feel this way is to take a few deep breaths, and relax. Look at the whole picture of what needs to be done. Make a mind map[xiv] or a list and prioritize the steps you need to take to reach your goals.

Delete anything from your list that does not take you toward your goals. Be willing to tell others that you would love to help them, but you just don't have the time right now. Soften to your present capabilities and ask for help when and where you need it. Move forward with a clear intention of doing your very best without crossing the line into being overwhelmed, which is an impediment to your ability to be efficient and productive and can also affect the productivity of others. Once again, learn to focus and relax.

The last thing to notice is that the dark line on the outer edge creates a solid line with few or no openings. You will learn in the next category of Spiritual Indicators that our spiritual and intuitive support and awareness show here, in the outer edges of the upper and lower lips. Feeling overwhelmed can block you from spiritual connection and intuition.

The feeling of too much to do can be temporary or it can be chronic. It can be a depleting cocktail of emotions with a fairly simple remedy. As we learned to do with a Brain Dump, relax, focus on what you can do really well and delegate, defer or delete the rest. If you have a Challenge Line or a Journey Line, review those chapters in this book. Go get your energy back, because it is unmistakable that your talents and skills are in demand, and someone, even if it's just you, needs you to show up. Pull your power back and go after your goals with enthusiasm and creativity!

SPIRITUAL INDICATORS

So much in our lip prints speaks to our spiritual life, if indirectly, but the spiritual indicators get right down to the business of your relationship with God and Universal Spirit, or GUS, as my friend KC Miller calls it. Generally speaking, Spiritual Indicators are the exceptions to the rule that says missing color equals missing energy. Spiritual energy empowers you. It never depletes you.

SPIRITUAL RECEPTORS

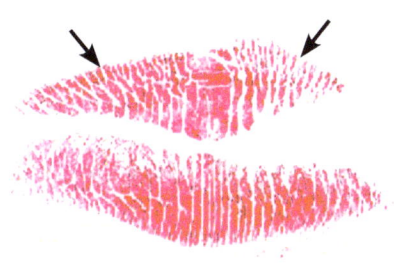

We naturally find the clearest indicators of our connection to Spirit at the highest point of the lips. Just as the crown chakra represents your connection to pure consciousness, the upper edge of the upper lip represents your interface with the same. Spiritual Receptors are white lines that come down into the upper edge of the upper lip and end in the interior of the lip, without cutting all the way through the lower edge (which would be a Gale Mark). They can be thought of as open receptors, similar to the receptors we have on each cell of our bodies. A cell's receptor receives signals and directs the cell to do something. When we have spiritual receptors we are open to receiving information that can guide us towards greater wisdom and awareness and help us make spirit-guided choices.

If you believe as I do, that there is more to our existence than the physical dimension and thought, then these lines are the calling card of that non-material dimension that surrounds and fills us. These lines represent your connection to the dwelling place of Divine Consciousness, the place to which we turn when we pray. From this Source we receive wisdom, insight, inspiration and creativity. When we have open receptors, there is an easy and available flow between that dimension and ourselves. We have more conscious access to the inner voice that speaks to us with wisdom, the wise grandfather if you will, who we all have in our hearts.

We learned earlier that thoughts show as lines before they bloom into emotionally depleted faded bands. The missing color in mental lines indicates lost or unavailable energy. Yet, the white lines of spiritual thought represent a supply of energy coming into the luminous field of a person. Spiritual thought has the potential to override mental thought and fill the void that is left with energy and illumination.

ANGEL MARKS

Now and then, you'll see a larger opening on the upper edge of the upper lip that looks like a wedge or a chunk that is missing.

When Jilly Eddy was doing her research, she found that many people with this indicator felt that they had an Angel on their shoulder, and so she called it an Angel Mark.

People who believe in angels are always delighted to hear that they have an angel nearby. If the mark is on the right, the angel is on the right shoulder. If it is on the left, the angel is on the left shoulder, because lip prints are not mirror images. Sometimes a client will immediately identify the angel. She may say, "Oh, that's my mother. I know she's looking over me." Some people believe in Guardian Angels, and they feel reassured to hear that they have evidence of their presence. If you don't believe in angels, you might think of this mark as amplified receptivity to Universal Consciousness and Knowledge, or possibly coming from one's higher self, or whatever higher level of consciousness to which you relate.

I am always quick to stress that just because one person has an Angel Mark and another does not, this does not mean that the second has no angels. If one of us has angels, we all have angels! (No need for angel envy!) But sometimes, they show themselves in a lip print because they want to get our attention about something, or just to let us know that they are there, and that we are loved! Or, it could be that the owner of the lips is proactively interacting with her angels in a conscious and intentional way as you'll see in the next example.

If you have Angel Marks, be on the alert for messages in the form of flashes of insight. You may feel inspired to say something or to take an action that will be of benefit to yourself or others. As my friend KC Miller says, when an angel whispers in your ear, pay attention! Just like the rest of us, an angel prefers to talk to someone who is listening!

THE HAND OF GOD

Not long ago, I was fortunate enough to be given the lip prints of the aforementioned beautiful and dynamic spiritual teacher, KC Miller. KC's on-line bio describes her as: Therapist, Teacher, Life Coach, Author, Entrepreneur and Ordained Minister, but she most prefers "Instrument of Spirit." KC owns two successful schools in Tempe, Arizona. The first is the Southwest Institute of Healing Arts, or SWIHA, where students can enroll in classes in Massage Therapy, Yoga Teacher Training, Holistic Nutrition, Western Herbalism, Bodywork, Life Coaching, Hypnotherapy and more. The second school is the Southwest Institute of Natural Aesthetics, or SWINA, where students learn state-of-the-art skin care and facial protocols, as well as a variety of spa treatments. KC is an inspiration and a role model for many, including me.

Print 161: KC Miller

She is the foremost teacher of Toe Reading and has an international contingency of Toe Reading students and graduates in Japan.

Print 161 is her lip print.

I was not surprised to see that she is a Diamond Girl. I expected that she would have Cheerleader energy, as she is high-powered, productive, optimistic and active.

The surprise for me was the size of the large Angel Mark on the upper left side of her first print. In fact, I decided to give this indicator a new name. I call it the Hand of God.

It reminded me of the scene from the old movie, *The Ten Commandments* when God parted the Red Sea for Moses. To me it resembles the dark shape that descends from the heavens and parts the waters. In the movie, they called it the "Breath of God."

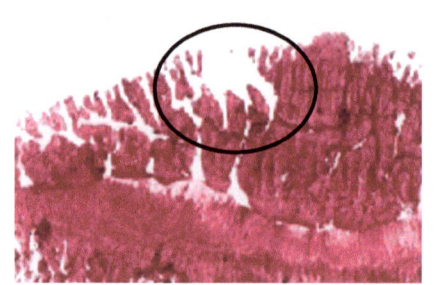

Print 162: The Hand of God and Islands

It came to me that this large delta (Print 162, an enlarged portion of Print 161) representing Higher Consciousness moving into her lip was an indication of how deep and actively articulate her relationship with God is.

And then, she has these interesting islands that are within the boundaries of her lip line, but seem to be separate at the same time. My intuition tells me that these represent the Archangels that she works with. KC is vocal and unabashed about her relationship with God and with Angels. When I spoke about this proactive relationship and interaction she has with God and the Angels, she confirmed my interpretation.

So, the Hand of God, I believe, is a mega-Angel Mark, and it represents a consciousness that is open and in an active, ongoing personal conversation with Spirit.

LINES OF INTUITION (MOTHER NATURE LINES)

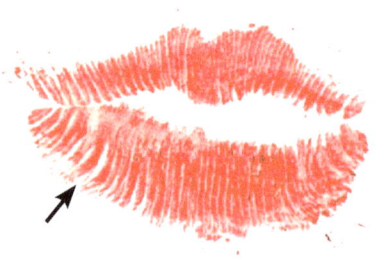

Print 163: Lines of Intuition

Just as the upper edge of the upper lip represents our interface with God, angels, and spiritual support, the lower edge of the lower lip print represents our resonance with the vibrational field of Mother Earth. Lines that move upward into the lower lip and end inside the lip are called Lines of Intuition. They represent intuitive receptors, as if you have your ear to the ground, and you can hear the sounds and vibrations of things coming your way.

When you are tuned into the planet, you will pick up feelings, sensations, and notions about what's going on around you. You'll be in tune with the songs of the plants, the waters, the stones and minerals, and with the oneness of life. You will feel the balance or imbalance of energy around you. You will be able to read people and to know things of which others are not aware. You will respond to your environment and to the people you meet with compassion and connection.

Grounding yourself in Mother Earth will enhance your vision. This is why some of the ceremonies of aboriginal people must be done outside. They believe as I do, that we do not own this world, but that we belong to it. We come from it, just as all creatures, plants, stones, waters and air emanate from the power and fecundity of our mother, this planet of Earth.

The more you resonate with the embrace, support and love of the fertile one who gave birth to you and to all of your ancestors, the more in tune you will be with your intuition and your gut feelings. The lines that come up into your lower lip represent your receptivity to the messages that are all around you. Because most people with lines of intuition enjoy being outside, these are also called Mother Nature Lines.

PSYCHIC WEDGES

Like its sister the Angel Mark, a Psychic Wedge represents wide open receptivity. In this case we see connection to the intuition and instinctive knowing that is always available if we are listening for it. Psychic Wedges are Lines of Intuition amplified. They show heightened support and information being funneled into your field of consciousness. Often, the individual with a wedge does indeed have psychic abilities, or at least, she has the potential to develop them.

Print 164: Psychic Wedges

Print 164 comes from a man who is the year-round caretaker of 60 acres of land in northern Arizona. He spends most of the year alone, tending the land with a noticeably deep reverence for "his piece of the garden". The land is used for an annual Sundance ceremony and for a handful of ceremonial gatherings throughout the year.

Print 165 belongs to a respected teacher of the ways and beliefs of Turtle Island, a name for the indigenous peoples of the western hemisphere. Notice that both of these men

SPIRITUAL INDICATORS | 195

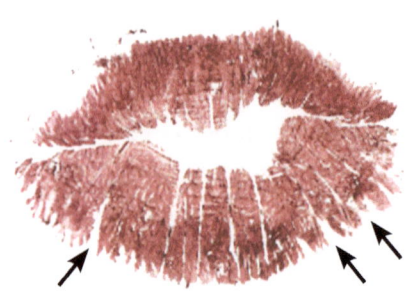

Print 165: Psychic Wedges

Print 166: Empathic Wedge

"drink" their spiritual support more through the straws of intuition and gut feelings than the upper spiritual receptors. Make no mistake that Lines of Intuition and Psychic Wedges represent access to spiritual energy and support just as powerfully as the northern Spiritual Receptors do.

The difference between the energy of the upper lip receptors and the lower lip receptors can be understood this way. The upper lip represents the channeling of information from the expanse of Intelligent Consciousness, like being bathed in rain water as it falls from the skies. It comes to us directly from the dimension of the formless. The lower lip receives information that is more grounded, more instinctive. Like water bubbling up from underground, it is filtered through the resonance of Mother Earth, the dimension of form. In every moment we are receiving insight through our heart and through our gut . . . it all comes from Spirit and it's all good.

I have noticed that the location of the wedge can be significant. For example, those with a Psychic Wedge on the very bottom of their lip, or what would be the South on a compass, seem to be natural empaths. (Print 166) A person with this southern wedge seems to be able to read the emotions and feelings of others, especially those she cares for. She will need to know how to protect herself from the world of emotions swirling around her, or she will be constantly pushed and pulled by the drama of others.

I feel certain that the locations of Angel Marks and Psychic Wedges will offer us additional insights as we gather more information.

ANGEL WINGS

My husband is a busy man. He has four businesses that he runs from his home office. If he didn't work at home, I wouldn't see much of him. He is often at his desk well before dawn, working past ten at night. When he is out in the field, he may not come home until after midnight. And yet, he can be found at many of my Lip Print Reading events, assisting men and women with their Kiss Cards and managing the line of people waiting for me. He's grabbing a plate of food for our drive home, and helping me break down my table and pack up at the end of the night.

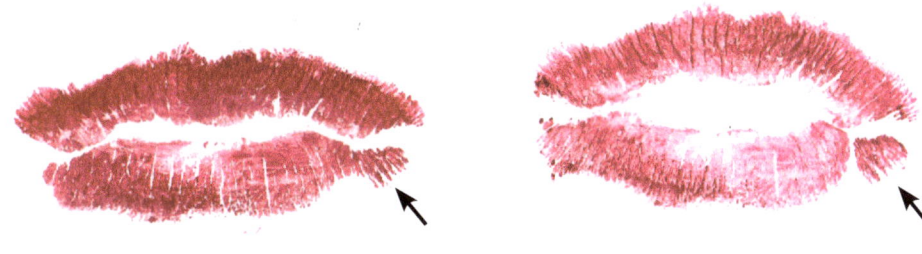

Jim's Angel Wings

Jim has Angel Wings, one of my favorite indicators! Angel Wings look like fluffiness at the corner of a print. They are usually on the lower lip, but can occur on the upper lip as well. Unlike Angel Marks, which remind us that we have support from the upper realms of consciousness, Angel Wings refer to the owner of the lips. They represent the good-natured generosity and thoughtfulness of the person who made the prints. This is someone who never shows up empty-handed at a party, or who brings a box of treats to work, the Dad who coaches his son's baseball league, the mom who surprises her daughter with a new pair of shoes, the friend who offers to drive you to the doctor.

All of these folks may be suspected of sporting Angel Wings, just as Jim does. There isn't a day that goes by that I couldn't name 20 thoughtful things that he did for me in the course of the day, as busy as he is. He is an angel right here on Earth and there are more of them around than you would imagine!

Print 167: Angel Wings

Print 167 is from a news journalist who interviewed me for a segment on a local TV show. He is funny, warm, creative and smart, and wonderful to work with. He was careful to make me look good and to edit the piece so that it was entertaining and fun. When I saw his Angel Wings before the segment aired, I felt comfortable that he would be kind to me in his representation of what I do, even though he had just met me.

Print 168 is from a local businessman who lives in my town. His wife hired me to do readings at his birthday party. The first thing I noticed about him

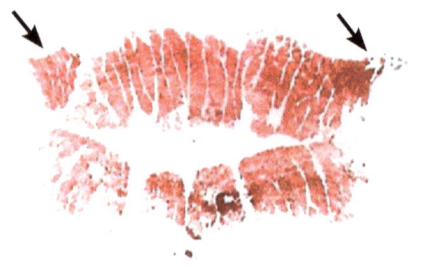

Print 168: Upper Angel Wings

when he sat down with me was the twinkle in his eyes. He has an air of mischief and playfulness. Those upper Angel Wings bring to mind words like "puckish," "merry," and "sprightly." All of these adjectives could describe this man, who was having the time of his life showering his friends with his humor, warmth, and hospitality that evening.

People with Angel Wings are often guilty of random acts of kindness, and I make sure these folks know what a treasure they are to those who are blessed to know them.

HELPING HANDS

Print 169: Helping Hands

Print 170: Helping Hands

Recently I began noticing this indicator that looks like a cupped hand at the corner of a lip print (Prints 169 and 170). I saw it in the prints of several people I knew. I had a hunch about what it might signal about a person, and I have validated it with clients of mine whom I have since read.

The Helping Hands indicator is a cross between the Zinger and an Angel Wing. As such, it suggests the speaking of one's opinion (Zingers) combined with an intention to be helpful (Angel Wings).

People who have Helping Hands corners are inclined to offer their directions and suggestions to others, sometimes in the form of unsolicited advice, with a sincere desire to help others become their highest potential. As such, they are natural mentors, and often feel that they have a calling to motivate those around them.

SEEDS OF TRANSFORMATION

When color is missing in the lower lip and the shape of the missing color is similar to a circle or an oval, we call this a Seed of Transformation. This is another exception to the rule of "missing color equals missing energy." What it says about the owner of the lips is that he is being called to a life of service. He is someone who can change the lives of many other people in positive and powerful ways. If the subject is young and not already aware of this pathway of purpose in her life, your reading of this indicator may actually plant a "seed of transformation" and open up new thought systems for her. But usually, people know or suspect that this is true about them, and the validation serves to affirm them in their life's purpose.

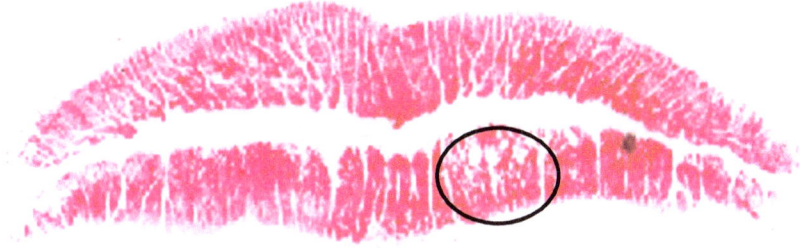

Print 171: Seeds of Transformation

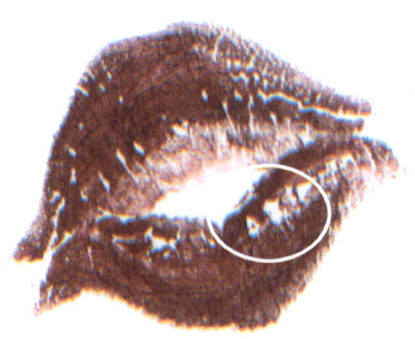

Print 172: Seeds of Transformation

Example 171 is the print of a spiritual teacher. She leads four day workshops all over the world. In addition she and her partner have journeyed several times to the Himalaya Mountains, delivering simple but safe cooking stoves to the Sherpa people. She has indeed helped to transform the lives of many.

Print 172 belongs to a TV newscaster. She is active in her community and is certainly in a position to transform the lives of those who watch her on TV.

Print 173: Seeds of Transformation

Print 173 belongs to a woman who has created a dynamic networking organization. She holds special events based on a theme, where people can come and network for work or for fun. People meet, they form professional or personal relationships and lives are changed.

Seeds of Transformation, while not common, are not overly rare. It is inspiring to notice how many of us are committed to leaving things a little better than they were when we got here.

STARBURST

There are some people who have a magnetism about them. They are attractive in ways that are noticeable. It may be their good looks, or their humor. They are people whom others admire and want to be around. Marilyn Monroe had it. Beyoncé has it. Ryan Gosling and Melissa McCarthy have it, and so do Justin Timberlake and Jimmy Fallon. Name a politician or corporate leader you admire. He or she has it, too.

But you don't have to be a celebrity to be a superstar. Look around your social circle. There are people you enjoy spending time with, and in fact, would spend more time with if you had the opportunity. It's very possible that those people and all of the ones I mentioned would have a Starburst in their lip prints.

A Starburst can be a round white spot, similar to a Seed of Transformation, or it can actually have lines radiating from it, like the rays of the Sun. Sometimes there are several, and sometimes, just one bright spot.

Print 174: Starburst

It doesn't show in every print, but when you see this in even one print of a set, it confirms the Superstardom of the person. You may be surprised on whose lips you'll see this "gold star" of an indicator. That's what makes the Starburst so transformational for the reader. It will remind you that we all have the ability to shine, and that there are people all around us who can inspire us in unexpected ways.

Our examples here are, first, my great-niece. (Print 174 and Image 175) She's been a star since she was a baby. Nowadays, she is a dancer, and a straight A student who volunteers at an animal shelter. She hopes to be a fashion journalist in the future.

This next print belongs to JC Scott, one half of the JC and Laney duo (Prints 176 and 177). JC is a singer/songwriter with a powerful and magnetic personality. The songs he writes and the beautiful harmonies of the duo's performances are spell-binding.

Image 175: Starburst in Action

JC has had a storied life. He lived in California in the LA music scene for many years before he met Laney. She became a stabilizing force in his life and literally brought balance and harmony with her. Now they seem to be on their way to stardom. With those Starbursts in his upper lip, I have no doubt that they will achieve their musical goals!

Image 176: JC and Laney

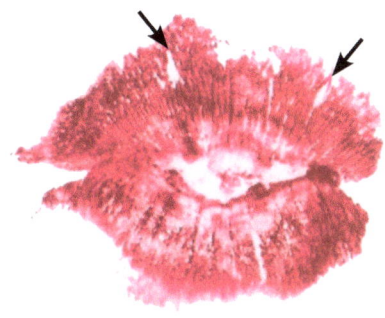

Print 177: JC's Starburst

SPIRITUAL INDICATORS | 201

Print 178: Marion Meadows
Starburst

The third example (Print 178) is the lip print of Marion Meadows (Image 179), an internationally acclaimed saxophone player who began studying classical music at the age of 8. His performances are mesmerizing and his music is transcendent. I'll let his picture speak for itself.

A Starburst in a lip print does not necessarily show up in someone who is already a star. It doesn't presuppose that the person will be a star in the cultural sense of a performer or someone who is extremely successful. It does mean that the person will shine and sparkle in ways that are noticeable to others.

Our lip prints affirm and support us. If we have an indicator, it is because we need to know or experience validation regarding something about ourselves.

Your Starburst wants you to know that you are meant to shine. You naturally attract the support of those around you, who admire you and wish you well.

You should know, further, that the heavens have sent a sign. As a person with a Starburst you have a purpose in this life, and that is to be an example of a life well lived, and to serve others by reminding them that we are all special in our way. Like the Diamond Lip Print, you are being asked to be a role model and a mentor to others. Be willing to help others see their own magnificence, even as you light the way with your own sparkling beauty.

Image 179: Marion Meadows

ANGEL DUST AND INTUITIVE MIST

Jilly and I had a conversation one day about the bits of color that are within the orbit of a lip print, but are not attached. Because we believe that the messages in our prints are not random, but rather that they come from some inner source of wisdom that is

Print 180: Angel Dust

Print 181: Intuitive Mist

proactively communicating with us, we decided to stay open to an inquiry about what these bits and pieces might suggest.

Now and then I see something that looks like a mist of particles above the upper lip and below the lower lip. Naturally we can deduce that the fine hairs around the lips of a woman and the coarser hairs of a beard on a man have created this, but that's no different than any other factor, like chapped lips or having had two glasses of wine when you made the prints. The message is always the message for that particular moment.

My feeling about Angel Dust and the Intuitive Mist are that they show an enhanced connection to Spirit or creativity. Like splashing in the waves lapping on the shore, we can step into this field and be bathed in its energy and guidance.

Print 180 belongs to a man who lives in Sedona, Arizona. His spiritual life is of primary importance to him. Before a career, before romantic relationships, before the material, he places his spiritual growth before everything else in his life. He is soft spoken, gentle and playful, fond of communing with nature on solitary hikes in Red Rock Country.

Print 181 belongs to a musician of Maori descent. Her name is Mihirangi. She has been trained since childhood in the traditions and culture of her ancestors, the indigenous people of New Zealand. Her lip prints have this Intuitive Mist, showing a deep spiritual connection to nature. Her original music is powerful, earthy, and hauntingly melodic. Her performances seduce and enfold you in the luxuriant vibrational connection she has to her music and the messages of her lyrics. She is also a spiritual teacher of Maori traditions and culture who can trace her genealogy back 25 generations. There is no doubt that she dances in the vibrational field of her intuitive connection to the living planet. Notice also that she has a Starburst in her upper lip!

There is more to learn about the messages of the satellites sometimes found orbiting around prints. Stay tuned!

PASSIONATE/CREATIVE INDICATORS

It's the Passionate/Creative energy body that had us making colorful crayon drawings in the first grade and proudly bringing them home from school for our Moms to admire. When puberty hit, some of us channeled a substantial amount of our creative energy into an obsession with the opposite (or same) sex, with crushes, fantasies, longings and desires, until we grew old enough to begin engaging sexually. Sexual energy is the twin sister of creative energy. After all, what is more creative than making another person?

For teenagers who can focus and direct the surging hormones in their bodies toward productive expressions, those early years of puberty can be very creative ones. I once heard puberty called the "veil of hormones" that descends upon us and becomes the filter through which we see our world. Throughout our lives we are compelled to express ourselves in creative ways. When we are teens, our innate nature urges us to reproduce ourselves . . . perhaps through procreation. When that is not an option because of cultural, moral, or actual restraints, we reproduce ourselves through works of art, music, technology, writing, cooking, woodworking, sewing, gardening, and all of the wonderful non-sexual ways we can find to be creative and self-expressive. Think of the computer nerd who could never get a date, but who puts all of his pubescent creativity into creating new technology in his parents' garage.

As we mature out of the teen years into our 20's and 30's, our hormones come into more balance and we build on our talents, supported by our creative energies. We raise our families, amass our material wealth, and define ourselves professionally. Gradually, as we continue to age, the non-sexual creative energy may begin to out-weigh the sexual energy. Post–menopausal women may find that they are once again focused on the dreams of youth. They may take ballet classes, or learn to paint or play the piano . . . goals they had as a girl, and now have the time and opportunity to pursue. The veil of hormones lifts, but the creative urge is still there.

This energetic body is like all of the others, in that it needs to be fed and nurtured in some way every day. The old axiom, if you don't use it you'll lose it almost applies. I think it's more that if you haven't used it you may have misplaced it. It is still somewhere nearby, and the way to recover your passion and creativity is to be proactive about stimulating that part of yourself. Take a class in drawing, dancing or cooking. Keep a daily journal. Make an effort to bring some romance back into your marriage. Just the process of finding ways to be creative is an act of creativity.

PASSION

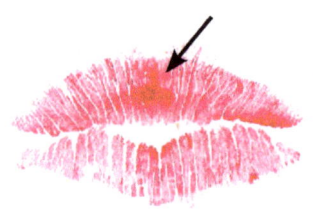

Print 182: Passion.

The Passionate aspect of this energetic body is most evident in the Hug Pucker and the Gourmet Lip Split areas (The Circle of Romance). The set of three lip prints in Print 182 gives us a good look at how this energy is displayed.

These prints were made at a meeting I was having with a new friend. She wanted me to read her lip prints and her questions were all about her relationship with her husband. She told me that they were living separately, but trying to work things out. She is gorgeous and very successful. He lives near me in a beautiful home. She talked about the differences they had when it came to life-style, his relationship with his daughters, and that darned motorcycle that he loved to ride!

I could see in her prints that the relationship was a passionate one. Look at the deep color, even in the first print, in the Hug Pucker. There is extreme energy in how she feels about him and how she is communicating with him. First we see a holding back (fading in the lower Hug Pucker) and then an aggressive, outward pushing of her thoughts and feelings. The Gourmet Lip Split, just below, is also highly charged indicating an intensity of connection. Even as the rest of the relationship was depleting her, her physical/emotional attraction to him was making it difficult to move on.

CREATIVITY

As we learned previously in the Irregular lip print shape, non-sexual creative energy can show as a general undulation or irregularity of the outline of the lip print. The three lip prints on the Kiss Card in Print 183 belong to a fine artist in Scottsdale, Arizona. Notice the "Elvis Lip" in print one, where the upper left side of the lip reaches up. The

Print 183: Kiss Card Revealing Creativity

angles and turns continue around the outline of the lip. In print three, you'll see the opposite side of her upper lip almost erupting like a bubble rising to the surface, as if there is something in there that needs to get out!

You'll also see creative energy in extremely extended information funnels, especially if they are energized. These are the curious creators.

Print 184: Curious Creativity

The prints in Print 184 were made by an attorney at a large Phoenix law firm. His Information Funnels and Eddys display a larger-than-life curiosity. The undulating pattern around his lip line indicates an ability to process the data, facts and clues that he gathers for his clients in ways that are creative and surprising.

Print 185: Curious Creativity

Print 185 belongs to a multi-talented southern gentleman who rose from classic middle class beginnings to become the CEO of an international manufacturing firm. He enjoys remodeling 19th century homes and vintage cars and decided in his retirement to raise pecans in the countryside of Breaux Bridge, Louisiana.

Print 186: Curious Creativity

Print 186 is one you have seen previously. He is a spiritual teacher who has studied with a number of Far Eastern and American masters. He is always seeking to learn more, so that he can teach more. His sermons and seminars are spirited, unique and inspiring, presented with heart and creativity.

Creativity shows in the "explosive" outlines that some lip prints make, such as these prints of a 5 year-old boy (Print 187) and a corporate executive. (Print 188)

Print 187: "Explosive Creativity"

Print 188: "Explosive Creativity"

DANCING LIP PRINTS

Another indicator I've noticed in musically creative people is the "Dancing Lip Print". You'll notice a humorous and lyrical bounce to the pattern of the prints.

Dancing Lip Prints are not laid down in a linear pattern across the Kiss Card. They will, however, seem to be attached at the corners by an invisible string running through their corners, like bows on the tail of a kite! The less acute the angles between the corners, the more we are seeing Dancing Lip Prints.

The first example (Print 189) here is the Kiss Card of the glamorous and charismatic lead singer of a 10-piece variety band. She is also a part-time member of an internationally acclaimed "Sister" act. Just as she dances onstage, her prints dance across the paper.

Print 189: Dancing Lip Prints

Next we have the Kiss Card of another musician, (Print 190) a singer-songwriter-poet who sings her whimsical songs in online videos as she strolls, and bounces a little, through woods and meadows with her dog.

Print 190: Dancing Lip Prints

Here are the prints of two more musicians who are a married couple and who have a successful dance band. They did not make these Kiss Cards in the presence of each other. They both just naturally and individually danced across their Kiss Cards! She (Print 191) is the dynamic lead singer who whips up the audience with her take-no-prisoners vocal style and dance moves as her husband (Print 192) plays bass guitar behind her.

Print 191: Dancing Lip Prints

Print 192: Dancing Lip Prints

Don't mistake Dancing Lip Prints for the "Tipsy Lip Print", which we see in the prints of someone confronting fears or disturbances in his or her life.

Imagine that kite string. Is it flowing and undulating in the breeze, or is it jerking and snapping, like a flag in a wind storm? The energies behind the undulation and the jerkiness are polar opposites. In our dancing musician's model, there is a rhythm to life that we can dance and "get down with."

When we balk and stagger, fighting the flow of change with fear and resistance, we get Tipsy Lips. Like leaves being blown by turbulent winds, Tipsy Lips suggest someone who believes she is at the mercy of her situation. (Print 193)

Print 193: Tipsy Lip Prints

You don't have to be a stage performer to have Dancing Lip Prints, but if you are not, you'll still be someone with a lyrical spring in your step!

Dancing lip prints show a creative mind that is willing to navigate the currents of life and take responsibility for the quality of the ride!

SYMBOLS

Sometimes when you look at a lip print, you may see something that looks like a tiny picture, or writing of some sort. I don't recommend poring over each print to see if you can spot something mysterious embedded in it. But if something jumps out at you and you notice it right away, I would say, give it your attention.

Here are some examples of symbols I have felt moved to discuss with my clients.

Lip Print 194 belongs to a vivacious woman named Liz Dawn who started a three-day weekend event called Celebrate Your Life with her mother years ago. It has turned into a highly successful gathering that attracts the most prominent writers and spiritual leaders in America. Keynote speakers include Marianne Williamson, Deepak Chopra, Dr. Andrew Weil and Dr. Wayne Dyer. She has also initiated a writer's workshop along with a well-known publishing house that publishes self-help, personal growth and spiritually related books. The publisher offers to publish the book of one participant at each workshop.

Print 194: Liz Dawn's Snow Goose

Print 195: Liz Dawn's Snow Goose

When I looked at her print, I was struck by the image of a snow goose (Print 195) in the right corner. The snow goose is a totem that assists in communication, especially the written word. It is so interesting to see it in the east of her lip print, the direction on the Medicine Wheel where spiritual growth sits, so that the symbol and the location together represent the confluence of writing and spirituality. Seems like the perfect symbol for what Liz is bringing into reality!

In this next example (Prints 196 and 197), I see a fetus-like shape in the lower lip. The owner of the lips is an eloquent educator who is innovative in his approach to teaching others how to achieve more, live more inspired lives and fulfill their most meaningful goals. He might be viewed as a "mid-wife" of sorts to those he mentors. I believe that this symbol in his print suggests that he is in the process of creating a dynamic and far-reaching vision that is still taking form. In fact, he speaks of leaving a legacy that would last a thousand years. That's a pretty big legacy to birth! His vision is to conceive and deliver the seed of a new mode of thinking and create a new era in self-governance and self-mastery in generations of people throughout the world.

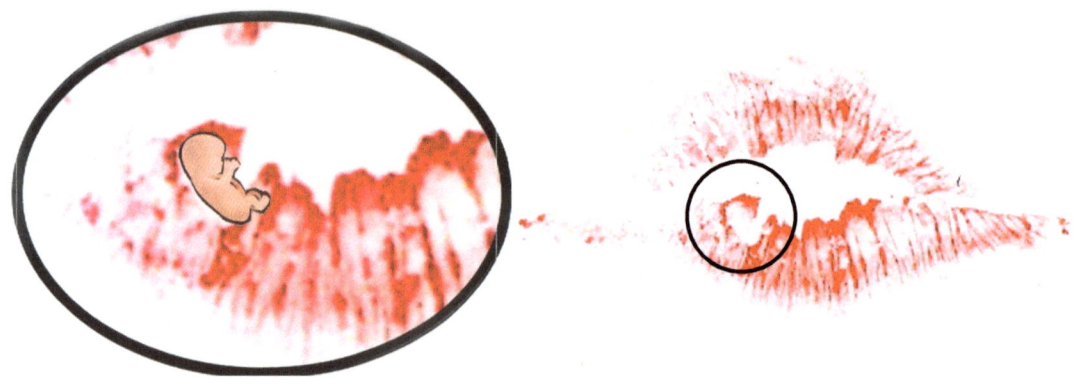

Print 196: Symbol of "Gestating Transformation"

Print 197: Teacher Creating a Legacy

The next example (198 and 199) had an image in it that popped out when I first looked at it. I was immediately reminded of a dragonfly. The dragonfly represents the grace of a dancer, as well as poise, power, presence, vision and change. The owner of this lip print was a dancer throughout her childhood and teens. Like all trained dancers, her posture is erect, strong and graceful. But the power you feel in her presence comes from the vision she holds that she can have a positive effect on her community.

She has worked with local Chambers of Commerce, school boards and a Texas State Representative to create change in her area for 40 years. In recent years she has headed a counsel dedicated to opening a career & technical high school that offers college credits and leads to immediate employment for graduates with local community businesses. Through fundraising efforts she raised $200,000 for the school in one year!

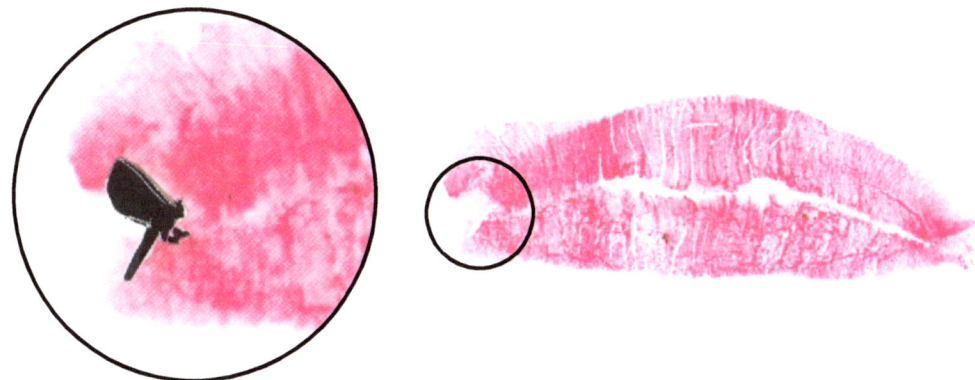

Print 198: Terrie's Dragonfly **Print 199:** Terrie's Dragonfly

If a dragonfly symbolizes vision, dreams made manifest, and grace then it's no surprise that one would show in this visionary woman's lip print!

And finally, Print 200 belongs to an eye surgeon.

Print 200: Eye Surgeon
with a Vision

The large white round spot on her lower lip is the first indicator that catches my eye when I look at this print. We talked about it being a Seed of Transformation. I explained that it suggested that she had a calling to transform and enhance the lives of others through her work. She looked at me with so much sincerity and said it is her goal to find a cure for glaucoma.

It was then that I realized that the round white spot with a dark dot inside resembled an eyeball! I feel confident she will indeed make a difference in the field of glaucoma research!

COMBINING INDICATORS

Once you have mastered your understanding of the personality and energetic indicators, you can begin to look at how these indicators combine to say even more about a person, to add a deeper dimension to your reading. Begin to access your intuition and consider what might come out of the blending of certain qualities.

For example, if your subject has both round and triangular shapes, spiritual lines and angel wings, you may be looking at someone who has natural healing talents, or who would be drawn to social work or the medical fields.

Someone with a full lower lip, a thin upper lip, open spacing and information funnels would likely be drawn to communications, broadcasting, public speaking or writing.

I read someone recently who had a Starburst, Seeds of Transformation, a Diamond shape, large lip prints, a Gourmet Lip Split. It was easy to see that she has been given the gifts of beauty, charisma, communication, humor, passion and an ability to move and inspire others. She is positioned by her beauty and capabilities to serve a high vibrational purpose, to follow a path of heart and to affect positive change in a larger community than her immediate circle of family and friends. It's up to her to find the vehicle through which she channels that purpose, but my job was to affirm for her the reality of her gifts.

I encourage you to use your intuitive abilities to notice how indicators combine to paint a comprehensive picture of the person you are reading. Allow the separate elements of the indicators to flow, merge, and blend together until you are able to perceive the beautiful mosaic of the Luminous Being in front of you. Then, when you see her in all of her shining, tell her what you see.

SAMPLE READING

Marion Meadows – Jazz Musician

Marion Meadows has been a musician since he was 8 years old. He is a saxophonist, composer, and smooth jazz recording artist. Mr. Meadows has released a total of nine albums to date.

I asked Marion for his lip prints on a day when he had just finished performing in a three hour concert with a beautiful jazz singer. With his open, spontaneous, win-win attitude, he didn't hesitate to say yes!

Marion Meadows
Lip Print Reading
Pam Fox ~ Lip Print Reader

Print # 1

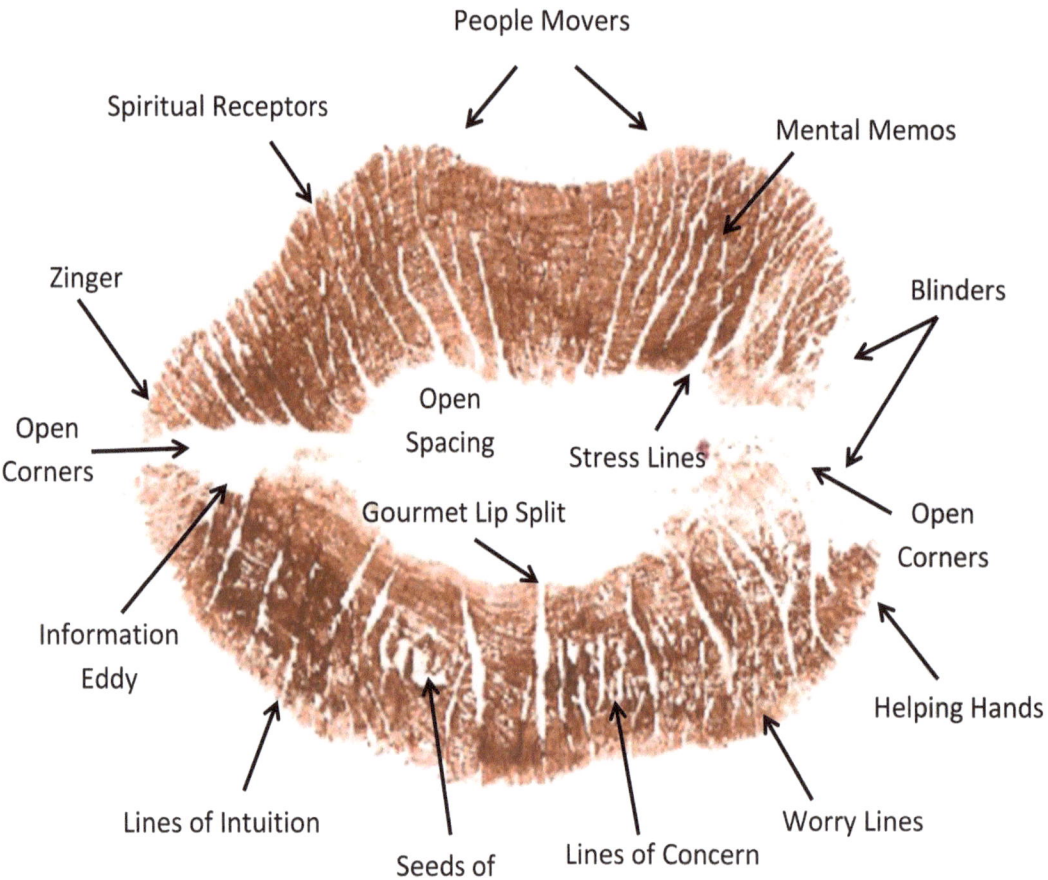

Labels around the lip print:
- People Movers
- Spiritual Receptors
- Mental Memos
- Zinger
- Blinders
- Open Corners (left)
- Open Spacing
- Stress Lines
- Open Corners (right)
- Gourmet Lip Split
- Information Eddy
- Helping Hands
- Lines of Intuition
- Worry Lines
- Seeds of Transformation
- Lines of Concern

SHAPE: Round/Square
FULLNESS: Medium to Full
COLOR: Intense
SPACING: Open/Open

LIPSTORY | 218

Marion Meadows
Lip Print Reading
Pam Fox ~ Lip Print Reader

Print # 2

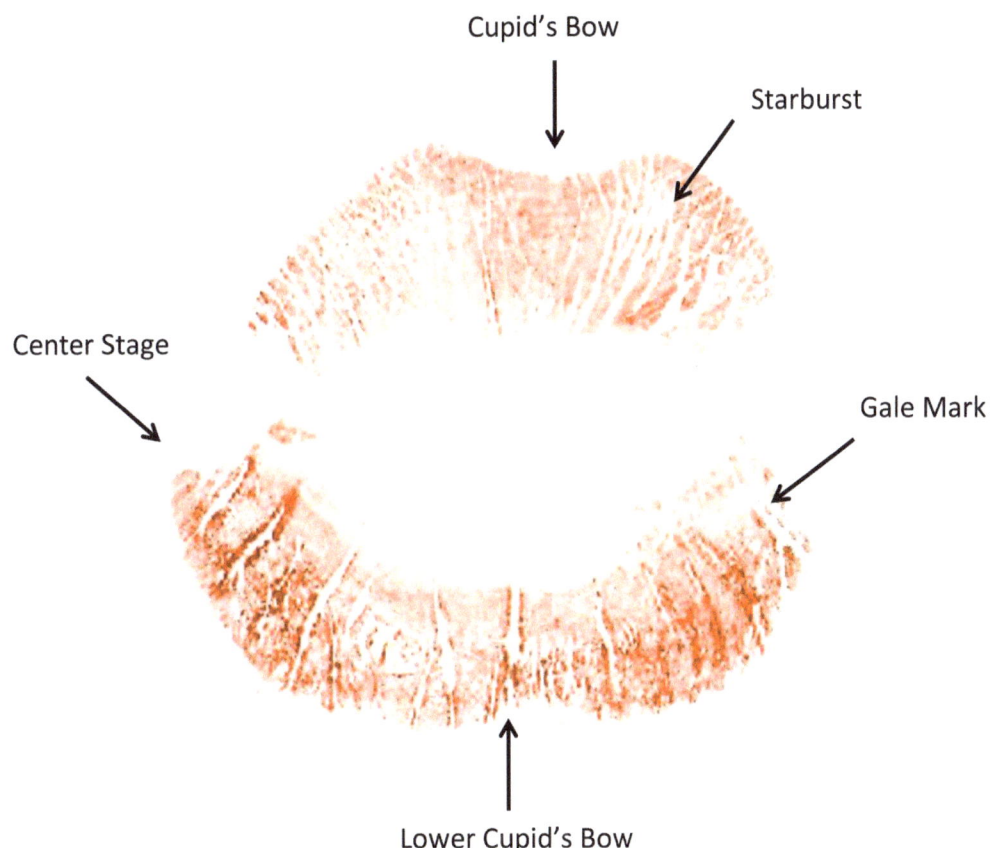

SAMPLE READING | 219

Marion Meadows
Lip Print Reading
Pam Fox ~ Lip Print Reader

Print # 3

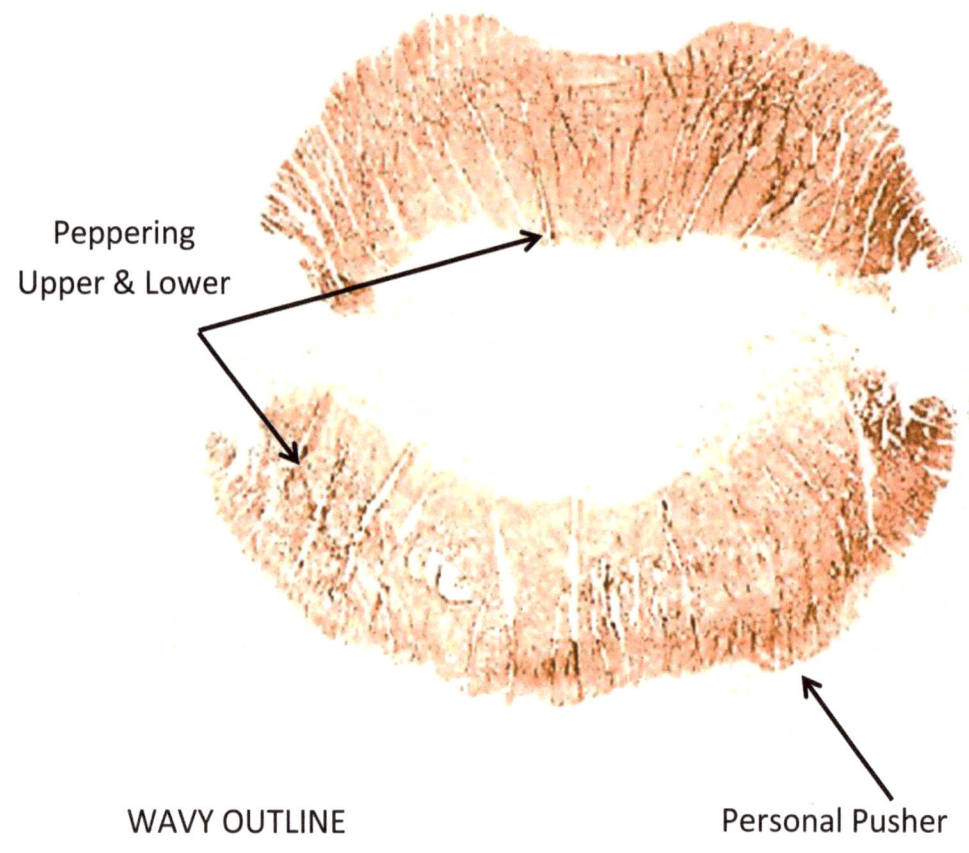

BLINDERS ~ "Missing," faded, or clipped off corners. When the corners are clipped off it's as though you have blinders on. You have some part of your corners missing in all three lip prints. You are intensely focused on the tasks at hand, but not in the most relaxed way. You may not be available to others or to yourself with so much focus on getting your to-do's done each day. Blinders ask you to stop and take a breath! Consider taking time off to reconnect with those around you, with yourself, and with your personal dreams.

CENTER STAGE ~ When the lower lip is wider than the upper lip, it signals that you are someone who is a role model and teacher for others. You are here to share your wisdom from center stage in ways that are far-reaching and beneficial. You inherently own an inspirational story that in the telling will inspire and uplift those who hear it. Learn to turn your personal experiences and earned wisdom outward toward the mentorship of others. This is what you are being called to do.

COLOR INTENSITY ~ Color equals energy in a lip print, with the exception of the indicators that have an asterisk*. Those indicators actually represent incoming energy. Your intensity indicates vibrant health on the day you made these prints. That's not to say that you weren't tired, but your underlying vitality was powerful.

CORNERS, SPACING and INFORMATION EDDY ~ your open corners and spacing show how willing you are to allow change and new adventures into your life. The circular space at the left corner of your first lip print says that sometimes you may get caught up in indecision and overthinking things a bit, but for the most part your open spacing says that you are usually ready to move on to the next new thing without much hesitation. There may be a tendency to be impulsive, and although your inner "Spirit Child" makes you an inspiration to others, your lips would ask you to take a breath and look before you leap into any big decisions! Also, you are easily bored and must have something going on or something to entertain or distract you most of the time.

CUPID'S BOW ~ The dip in the top of your upper lip is called a Cupid's Bow. It suggests that you care about what others think of you, that you will look for the win/win and that you seek balance and harmony around you, but not enough to give away what's important to you in any negotiation.

GALE MARK ~ A white line that cuts completely through a lip, upper or lower. Gale Marks represent storms that have blown through your life and devastated the landscape. If a line cuts all the way through your upper lip, other people are involved and you are still working through the consequences of the situation with another person or others. If it cuts through your lower lip, the struggle is internal, something you may not talk about, but that you do spend energy thinking about. As long as you have lines that cut through either lip, you have not yet learned the lesson the situation was there to teach you. You have several lines that on first glance appear to be Gale Marks, but if there is any speck of color in the white line, it is not a true Gale Mark. Still, there are one or two that qualify, so be patient with yourself if you find yourself rehashing past events, and remember to stay present and stay open to the teachings in those memories that are waiting like gifts to be opened.

INFORMATION EDDY ~ Circular space between the upper and lower lip on either corner, a place where information gets caught in a vortex of overthinking. See Corners.

FULLNESS ~ Indicates the scope of interest. Your lip prints are of medium to full width. The upper lip is the "listening lip" and the lower lip is the "communication lip." The fuller the upper lip, the more topics you are interested in listening to and learning about. With the tapered corners, evident on the left side of the first print, you will have a specialty and you will be focused and a perfectionist about it. Your lower lip shows a healthy and balanced ability to communicate easily with others.

GOURMET LIP SPLIT ~ The line or "v" shape in the center of the lower lip. This is a great indicator to have! It shows how social you are. It demonstrates a sense of humor and a high degree of charisma. People with this indicator are romantic and sensual. They love good food and usually like to entertain. The Gourmet Lip Split sits in the area of your lips where your appetites are displayed. When you have this mark you are someone who gives yourself permission to enjoy all of your appetites! You like the good things in life and feel happiest when you are surrounded by a beautiful environment, when you have your luxuries at hand, and when you can share them with others . . . who, by the way, love being in your company! Your GLS is showing a bit of stress, so it may be that you are worried about something in this area of your life.

HELPING HANDS ~ A cup like protrusion at the corner of the lower lip. These are similar to Zingers, but they indicate that you make suggestions to others that you hope will uplift them and help them evolve. It's one sign of a mentor, and reflects a desire to help others succeed.

LINES OF CONCERN ~ The internal lines in the lower lip are the precursors to full-blown worry, regret and lack of presence. See WORRY below.

***LINES of INTUITION** ~ Open lines on the lower lip that flow up into the lip, also known as Mother Nature Lines. These lines indicate that you enjoy being outside and that you are connected to the vibrational field of the planet in ways that feed your intuition and your gut feelings. You read people and situations well and sense what's coming your way.

LOWER CUPID'S BOW ~ An upward bow in the lower lip. For a man who has a lower Cupid's Bow, this indicator points towards his inner "female warrior." These men can also be emotionally expressive. A conscious connection to the inner warrior brings us pure intentions, focus, organization and relaxed authority. When a man is aligned with his inner warrior, we see his ability to stand in serenity in situations that require a presence of power without aggression.

When you have an upper and a lower Cupid's Bow you will have great skill in diplomacy. The fuller your lips, the better you will be able to charm others into agreement.

With both the Upper and the Lower Cupid's Bow, you will be empathetic, seeking the best course of action based on the desires and highest good of all parties while maintaining your integrity in the process.

MENTAL MEMOS ~ Lines that are internal to the upper lip and don't reach either edge. The lines that squiggle around in your upper lip represent mental distraction. Imagine a little secretary inside your head who writes a memo every time you say something to yourself that requires an action. It can be as simple as, "I want to try that new restaurant," or as important as, "I need to apply for a loan." If you haven't taken any action, the thought remains as an energetic byte of energy that interferes with your focus. The best cure for Mental Memos is a Brain Dump. Take a couple of days to let all of the open loops in your mind percolate to the surface and write them down. Much of what you write will be things you can cross off the list. Once you feel you have a complete list, delete all the unimportant items, defer what you need to, setting a time when you will take action, delegate what you can, and DO the rest. Once you have the list attended to in the 3rd dimension, your inner secretary can clean her desk and take a coffee break. And all of the missing energy represented by the white lines will return!

PEPPERING ~ Black specks in upper or lower lip. Peppering in the upper lip means that you were annoyed at someone or about something when you made the prints. Peppering in the lower lip is about your body needing some care and attention. It could be as simple as being dehydrated or tired. You HAD just performed in the heat for three hours!

PEOPLE MOVERS ~ Protrusions on the outer edge of the upper lip. Indicators of natural leadership abilities and ambition . . . a willingness to put yourself out there and to ask others to follow you.

PERSONAL PUSHERS ~ Protrusions on the outer edge of the lower lip. You set a high standard for yourself in ways that only you are aware of. It means a lot to you to achieve your goals. Be sure to acknowledge yourself when you do.

*SEEDS OF TRANSFORMATION ~ white circular spots on the lower lip suggest that you have a purpose in life, and it is to change the lives of others in powerful and positive ways.

SHAPE ~ Shape is the geometric figure we get when we draw a line around the outer edge of your lip print. Your lip prints are a combination of round and square. The shape of your lips speaks to how you present yourself to others, and how you are called to be of service. Very much like a wheel, the round print represents forward movement, going places, and reaching goals and destinations. The owner of this shape is someone who can motivate others to move towards the desired end result and towards completion. The fully self-expressed "Round" person works well with others, in fact depends on the team energy to succeed. The Motivator is an inspiration to others and although he seeks harmony and ease, when Zingers are present, he is not shy about "poking" others verbally to keep things moving.

The Round Lip Print is also the shape of one who accommodates others by supplying them with something tangible that they need to reach their goals. For example, Oprah Winfrey was expressing as a Round Lip Print when she built a school in South Africa for teenage girls. Habitat for Humanity is a Round Expression, but so is feeding your children, or donating clothes to Goodwill. Any time and any way that you are giving material support to others, you are in your "roundness" and it is a very authentic expression for you. Having your friends to dinner, fundraising, picking up office supplies at Office Max so a project can be completed are all expressions of tangible support. There are simple ways to express this shape and very big and complex ways. You have the ability to hold and fulfill an ambitious vision for yourself and those within the sound of your music!

The Square Lip Print is the shape of the Problem Solver. When you are Square, you are the go-to person that others rely on. You may hear yourself saying, "Don't worry . . . I got it." We call it the Godfather lip print, as you can make the problem go away. It's a powerful place to stand, as others depend on you. However, you need to set boundaries so that your generosity is not abused. Also, whenever you are helping others or allowing them to hand something off to you, be very clear about the distinction between empowering others or enabling them. You will be empowered when you empower others and depleted when you enable them.

*SPIRITUAL RECEPTORS ~ Lines that enter the upper lip from the top edge and do not go all the way through the lip. Think of these as open receptors that connect you to that dimension that we turn to when we ask for guidance, insight, inspiration and creativity. The energetic place from which we receive vision and wisdom is feeding and nurturing you when you have these open lines.

*STARBURST ~ Folks with this indicator in the upper lip, which can look like a sun with lines radiating off of it, have a natural charm and charisma, a magnetism, that makes other people want to be around them. When you have the Starburst, you are attractive in ways that are noticeable. People admire you and want to be like you. You have been given a stage in life from which you are asked to be a role model and to be a mentor. Being a role model is a passive thing. You need only remember to set a good example of a life well lived, and to earn and deserve the admiration that you are given. Being a mentor, on the other hand, is a pro-active position. When others come to you because they want to be like you, your job is to show them how they can shine in their own, unique way, and to help clear away any limiting illusions they may hold that stand in the way of their own success.

STRESS LINES ~ Lines that begin in the upper lip and flow out of the lower edge into the space between the lips. Like leaving all of your water faucets on at home, stressing about things that you cannot change or control is a waste of your resources. These lines represent energy leaving your "luminosity." When you are stressing, you are having an argument with reality, which you will lose. Practice owning your stress. It is your creation, and it is a choice, even when it is an unconscious one. You can make another choice. When you notice yourself stressing, say to yourself, "Stress is always a choice. I can choose differently." Then continue to stress if you want to, but know that it is costing you. Eventually, you'll see the insanity of spending energy on something and getting nothing in return. You will develop a mental muscle that will make it easier to disconnect from depleting thoughts and to direct your energy in more productive directions.

WAVY OUTLINE ~ A way outline indicates a creative personality. The undulating outline of the lips confirms your powerful creative talents.

WORRY /REGRET/DISTRACTION LINES ~ Lines in the lower lip that begin inside the lip and exit out of the top edge into the space between the lips. These lines can actually represent worry, regret, or distraction. Unlike Mental Memos, this kind of distraction has less to do with the outside world of "to-do's" and more to do with your inner world of desires, goals, insecurities, personal disappointments, and procrastinations. Whether these depletions come from spending time in an imagined future where things don't go the way you wish them to, or in a past where things didn't go the way you wanted them to, or in the present where you are not paying attention to where you are, they all represent you leaving the present moment and going to some imaginary place that does not exist. These lines are a message that you would benefit from some practice of mindfulness.

Remember this; nothing ever happens in the future. Things happen now when you can respond and make choices.

Whatever happened in the past was meant to teach you something. Like the blind man holding the tail of the elephant, you don't have the whole picture. Stay open to whatever is left to understand about past difficulties and stay present.

Notice when your mind wanders away from where you are. Being here, right now, is the hardest thing to do as humans, but right here and right now is where life is happening. Now is where the blessings are, where God meets us in the eternal present moment. Don't miss any more of it than you can help!

ZINGERS ~ pointed corners to either the upper or lower lips. Yours are not needle sharp, but are on the blunter side. Still, you are able to say what needs to be said to motivate those around you! These are one of the indicators of humor. The Gourmet Lip Split shows that you are funny, and so do Zingers. But Zingers are more an indicator of your intellectual wit, more of a way of poking people with your humor because you want them to cooperate with you. They represent humor with an agenda!

Where you shine:

You shine all over the place! You are a born star, and have been given the gifts of charisma, creativity, leadership and the ability to change the lives of others through your natural ability to solve problems and to work with others in harmonious ways (literally). You are one of the few people on this planet who knew from childhood what his purpose in life was, and you are using your gifts in ways that are transformative for others. Bravo, Marion!

Where you can stalk your energy:

Your lips are asking you to own your stress and to practice making another choice when you notice you are resisting reality. And there is a call for a practice of mindfulness. Seek resources, teachers, writings, videos or seminars that can guide you into a daily practice of mindfulness. You are living an extraordinary life . . . your lips don't want you to miss a moment of it!

IN CONCLUSION

Once you understand the fundamentals of it, Lip Print Reading is one of your most accessible tools for self-awareness. Checking in with the messages in your prints on a regular basis will give you direction and focus as you learn to honor your energetic bodies, to stay present and move forward on your life path with purpose and intention.

We have more to learn about our lip prints. I look forward to a shared on-going inquiry into the messages awaiting our understanding!

Wishing you many kisses,

Pam

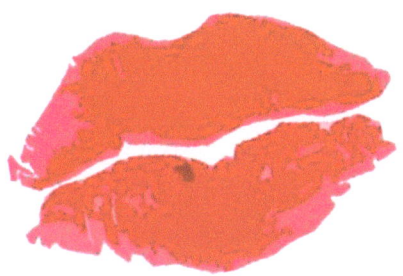

ABOUT THE AUTHOR

Pam Fox is one of a handful of Certified Lipsologists in the world. She is a keynote speaker on the subject and has appeared in interviews on ABC, NBC, CBS, The Travel Channel and several local TV stations in the Phoenix area. She has been invited to speak on radio programs as far away as South Africa. She is presently touring with a major cosmetic company at events nationwide.

Pam teaches professional Lip Print Reading, and is available for private readings and events. She continues to write books and articles, and is developing a line of products inspired by her desire to make lip print reading more accessible to the public.

Find her at www.LipStory.com and www.facebook.com/LipStory

ENDNOTES

[i] To learn more about Queen Puabi (aka Queen Shub Ad or Ur) go to: http://sumerian-shakeseare.com/117701/118101.html and http://www.penn.museum/sites/iraq/

[ii] For more in-depth information about the history of lipstick, try *Fashions in Make-up: From Ancient to Modern Times* by Richard Corson, and *Read My Lips: A Cultural History of Lipstick* by Meg Cohen and Karen Kozlowski

[iii] To read an online article about how much lipstick a woman eats in her lifetime go to: http://www.futurederm.com/2013/06/06/beauty-myth-busting-do-women-actually-eat-7-pounds-of-lipstick-in-their-lifetimes/

[iv] Read more about Edmond Locard at:
http://forensicsciencecentral.co.uk/edmondlocard.shtml
http://www.swissforensic.org/presentations/assets/aafslocard.pdf where you'll find a biography of Mr. Locard and suggested reading

[v] For more information on the history of cheiloscopy go to:
http://www.ncbi.nlm.nih.gov/pmc/articles/PMC3470419

[vi] *With Love From . . .*, published by A & W Publishers, Inc., New York, Copyright © 1980, Save the Children Fund

[vii] Read Jilly's story in her book *Lipsology, the Art and Science of Reading Lip Prints*, copyright 2014 by Jilly Eddy, Book Publishers Network

[viii] *Toe Reading; Are You Walking Your Destined Path?* Publisher: LuLu, June 2009, Available on Amazon

[ix] Read a fascinating article on this new technology at:
http://www.redorbit.com/news/science/1112926418/computer-reads-thoughts-using-mri-images-and-algorithm-081913/

[x] The book is *Hollywood Lip Prints: The Clay Campbell Collection, with Handwriting Analysis,* by Sidney Sheldon O'Connell. I highly recommend you read it, notwithstanding the uniformity of the prints. You'll still see indicators that sneak in to proclaim the individuality of their owners. It's an entertaining collection of pictures, autographs and prints from another time.

[xi] Luminous Being/luminosity: The spherical zone of energy that surrounds a person containing his/her local energy; i.e. the mental, emotional, physical, spiritual and creative energy bodies. Often experienced as "personal space."

[xii] The other two being: 1) Qi or Chi, the ambient energy we gather through breathing and eating; 2) Shen, the essence of consciousness, awareness, and love. It is the mind and the spirit of a person.

[xiii] See more about the concept of radiant health at: http://www.dragonherbs.com Click on "Herbalism and Philosophy."

[xiv] Mind Map - a visual map of a project with the main project in a circle in the middle and all of the tasks needed to complete it attached like spokes around the center word or phrase.

BIBLIOGRAPHY

Quotes within the Text

Page 27 - Dillard, Annie, *The Writing Life*, Harper Perennial, 1989

Page 49 - *Black Elk Speaks*, used with permission from SUNY Press, Rights and Permissions, 22 Corporate Woods Blvd, 3rd Floor, Albany, NY 12211

Page 80 - Kintz, Jarod, Nomadic Philosopher, American Humorist and Blogger—find him at http://jarodkintz.blogspot.com/

Page 99 - Meredith's story used with permission of her mother, Amy Hallsey

Page 106 - Bruce Lee Quotes at http://www.goodreads.com/author/quotes/32579.Bruce_Lee

Page 108 - Kuby, Lolette, *Faith and the Placebo Effect*, Origin Press, October, 2003

Page 116 - Sandberg, Sheryl, *Lean In*, 1st Edition, Knopf, 2013

Page 133- Kara, http://cheerleading.about.com/od/cheerquotes/a/030103a.htm

Page 157, 164 - Dillard, Annie, *Pilgrim at Tinker Creek*, Harper Perennial Modern Classics, 2007

Page 170 - Poet David Wagoner quote from *The Wisdom of Yoga: A Seeker's Guide to Extraordinary Living*, Cope, Stephen, a Bantam Book, 2006, page 18

Page 170 - Thich Nhat Hanh, *Living Buddha, Living Christ*, Riverhead Books. 1995

Page 185 - Lesson 7, *A Course In Miracles*, published by Foundation for Inner Peace, 1976

Permissions - Images

Fotolia, Cover image, and one variation on opening quote page, used repeatedly throughout the book

Page 15 - Queen Puabi, photo of Queen Puabi used with the permission of the University of Pennsylvania and the Penn Museum Archives, University of Pennsylvania Museum of Archaeology & Anthropology, 3260 South Street, Philadelphia, PA 19104 photos@pennmuseum.org T 215.898.8304 F 215.898.0657

Page 30, 31 - Photos of Tim Emerson and Slate Babineaux, (respectively) used with permission

Page 56 - Photo of the Pyramid of the Sun used with permission of owner

Page 57 - Photo of Teri Macias used with permission of owner

Page 68 - All photos used with permission. Thanks to Nelly in Rome, Eden in Toronto, Anthony in Sedona, and Jim

Page 77 - Photo of Anthony Mazzella, used with permission

Page 101 - Photo of Amy and Meredith used with permission

Page 139, 229 and back cover - Photo of Pam Fox by Harley Bonham, www.harleybonham.com, used with permission

Page 163 - Image of stressed woman, used with permission of owner

Page 201 - Picture of Gabriela Sol used with permission. Picture of JC and Laney, used with permission

Page 202 and 217 - picture of Marion Meadows used with permission

All lip print images are the property of the author.

GLOSSARY

Note: Where I have chosen to rename an indicator, I have included the original name given to it by Jilly Eddy, followed by an *.

ANGEL DUST - Caused by the fine hairs around the mouth, this looks like a sprinkling of dust above the upper lip, and indicates a playful and creative relationship with Universal Consciousness.

ANGEL MARKS - Wedge shaped divots in the top of the upper lip indicating an "angel on your shoulder."

ANGEL WINGS - A fluffy corner, usually on the lower lip, suggests a generous, thoughtful nature.

BFF LINE (KEEPERS*) - Dark lines on the inner edges of the lips seen on those who protect their inner circle of friends.

BLINDERS - Faded or missing corners show focus on tasking and disconnection from oneself and others during that focus.

BRAIN DUMP - A process of making a list by emptying all mental distractions onto paper and getting them out of your head. A Brain Dump is not complete until all items on the list have been attended to and crossed off.

CENTER STAGE - The lower lip is horizontally wider than the upper lip, indicating the potential for teaching from one's own experience.

CHALLENGE LINE - A band of faded color across the upper lip, showing a feeling of disappointment in a person or a situation.

CHEERLEADER LIP PRINTS - Prints with solid or near solid and intense color, found on energetic people whose enthusiasm can be charming and persuasive.

CIRCLE OF ROMANCE - The area encompassed by the Hug Pucker and the Gourmet Lip Split where indicators about close relationships are found.

CORNERS - The part of the prints indicating a person's need for information, his sense of caution or spontaneity, his ability to keep a confidence, his level of attachment to things, his style of speaking opinions, his thoughtfulness or lack of tact, his perfectionism and focus. A corner is closed if there is any color connecting the upper and lower lip, otherwise it is some degree of open.

CUPID'S BOW - A "V" shape that cuts down into the upper lip directly under the nose, indicates a desire for harmony and a willingness to negotiate.

DANCING LIP PRINTS - Prints that are not placed in a line, with corners that would connect smoothly without extremely sharp angles on a line running through the corners, often found on musicians and people who are have a lyrical perspective or who like to dance.

DROOPY LIPS - Prints with corners that turn down at the corners can signal a "glass is half empty" point of view.

ENERGETIC BODIES - The mental, emotional, physical, spiritual, and passionate/creative energy bodies that together make up the luminous body and field of energy of an individual.

ENERGIZED - Intense color, either in a line, an area or in the background color of a print.

FEATURES - Physical attributes of a lip, such as size, shape, Hug Pucker, Gourmet Lip Split, Cupid's Bow. They are also "indicators" of personality traits.

FIXED BELIEFS - Opinions that are not the truth that one nevertheless accepts and doesn't question.

FULLNESS - The width of a lip in a print demonstrating a person's focus from specialization (narrow) to a wide range of interests (full).

GOURMET LIP SPLIT - This line or indentation in the center of the lower lip on the upper edge is found on those with an appetite for all the good things in life, from food to friends and pleasing surroundings. It's a mark of humor, passion, generosity, charisma and pleasure taken in entertaining friends (with food).

HAPPY LIPS - Prints with corners that turn up suggest an optimistic nature.

HELPING HANDS - A cup-like protrusion on the corner of the lower lip is seen on people who offer unsolicited advice with a desire to be helpful.

HUG PUCKER - The area of the upper lip that is in the center on the inner (lower) edge of the lip. A prominent Hug Pucker is a fleshy orb in the center of the lip, but the area may be flat as well. We find information about the romantic nature of a person here.

HYBRID LIP PRINT - A lip print that resembles more than one geometric shape, for example, a round square.

INDICATOR - Markers in a lip print that represent the qualities of a person, such as color intensity, Zingers, Angel marks, Angel Wings, Seeds of Transformation, etc. Indicators also include the physical features of a print.

INFORMATION EDDY - A circular opening in an Information Funnel indicating a tendency to overthink.

INFORMATION FUNNEL - A V-shaped "entrance" or channel into the corner of a lip print showing the degree of curiosity or the need for information a person has.

INTUITIVE MIST - Stippling or smearing below the lower lip in a print showing a playful or creative interaction with one's intuitive abilities and an enhanced connection to the planetary vibration.

IRREGULAR LIP PRINT - A lip print that does not have a regular geometric outline, i.e., square/rectangular, round/oval, triangular, or diamond. It indicates creativity and can also represent moodiness or trauma.

JILLY EDDY - The Mother of Lipsology, author of *Lipsology, The Art and Science of Reading Lip Prints*. Jilly discovered the first 25 indicators in lip prints, and their variations, in 1990.

JOURNEY LINE (LOWER STRESS LINE*) - A faded band of color that runs horizontally across the lower lip indicationg a self-critical inner voice.

KISS CARD - Any paper, card, or page used to collect lip prints.

LINES OF CONCERN - White lines that are internal in the lower lip suggesting distraction due to procrastination and inaction.

LINES OF INTUITION (MOTHER NATURE LINES*) - Lines that come up into the bottom edge of the lower lip and terminate within the lip represent our interface with the vibrational field of the planet and our receptivity to intuition and gut feelings.

LINES OF WORRY, REGRET, DISTRACTION - White lines that exit the top edge of the lower lip denoting a lack of presence due to worry, regret or distraction.

LOCATION - The position of a print on the Kiss Card, the position of a feature or indicator, or the position of missing color.

LOWER CUPIDS BOW - An arch coming up into the lower edge of the lower lip. Its presence suggests an ability to stand one's ground with grace and flexibility.

LOWER HUG PUCKER - A protrusion in the center of the lower lip print on the top inner edge of the lip, showing an unspoken need for comfort either from others or through satisfying one's appetites.

LUMINOUS BEING/LUMINOSITY - The spherical zone of energy that surrounds a person containing his/her local energy; i.e. the mental, emotional, physical, spiritual, and creative energy bodies. Often expressed as "personal space."

MENTAL MEMOS (GERBIL WHEELS*) - Colorless lines inside of the upper lip showing mental distractions.

MISSOURI LIP PRINT - Completely closed or nearly closed lip print indicating a skeptical view of the opinions of others, dislike of surprises and an appreciation for traditions.

MOTHER HEN - Lip print in which the upper lip is wider than the lower or even extends over and around the sides of the lower lip. This is someone who has a natural ability for and takes pleasure in caring for and nurturing others.

PEOPLE MOVERS (PUSHING BARS*) - Upward pointing bumps or protrusions on the upper lip show ambition and leadership.

PERSONAL PUSHERS (PUSHING BARS*) - Downward pointing bumps or protrusions on the lower lip showing an inner drive and ambition that is not apparent to others.

PERSONAL UTILITIES - Same as the Energetic Bodies: mental, emotional, physical, spiritual, and passionate/creative.

PHYSIOGNOMY - Any method of looking at a part of the body to understand the whole person, and the outside of the body to understand the inner person.

POSITION - Where the lip print is placed on the Kiss Card.

POINTED BOTTOM LIP - The bottom lip comes to a point suggesting a focused, motivated, confident personality.

PSYCHIC WEDGE (OLD SOUL MARK*) - A large, usually V-shaped, opening on the bottom edge of the lower lip representing psychic abilities.

ROUND BOTTOM LIP - The rounded bottom lip (without Zingers) suggests helpfulness, congeniality, and a team player. Combined with a rounded top lip, this is a people person.

SEEDS OF TRANSFORMATION (SEEDS OF CHANGE*) - Round, white spots in the lower lip that indicate a calling to be of service in a transformational way.

SHAPES - There are five categories: round/oval, square/rectangular, triangular, diamond-shaped, and irregular. Your shapes define your most authentic way of expressing yourself in service to others.

SIZE - Small, medium or large; generally based on the width of the print, fullness and height. Size speaks to how one approaches work and relationships, both professionally and personally.

SPACING - The distance between the upper and lower lip in a print, or the vertical distance between the corners of a print. Spacing suggests a frame of reference on the world, from closed, private and cautious to open, spontaneous and adventurous.

SPIRITUAL RECEPTORS (SPIRITUAL LINES*) - Lines coming down into the upper lip and terminating inside the lip, representing receptivity to spiritual guidance and wisdom.

STARBURST - A star or circular white or faded area in the upper lip found on people with "star quality" and lots of charisma.

TIPSY LIPS (TOPSY-TURVEY LIPS*) - Prints that are in sideways or slanted positions, as if blown by the wind indicate someone who is feeling that some area of her life is uncertain, out-of-control, or chaotic.

ZINGERS - Pointed corners on lip prints indicating a propensity for speaking one's mind. The sharper the points, the more pointed the speaking. Zingers can indicate a sense of humor that is used to motivate or "poke" others, and it can be found on people who have little time to be tactful.

INDEX

A
Angel Dust; 202, 203, 235, 241
Angel Marks; 25, 192–193, 196–197, 235, 237
Angel Wings; 196–198, 215, 235, 237
Artsy Fartsy; 61–63

B
BFF Line; 109, 235
Blinders; 105, 106, 153, 221, 235
Brain Dump; 160, 190, 223, 235

C
Center Stage; 59, 127–128
Challenge Line; 178, 179–183, 189, 190, 235
Cheerleader Lip Prints; 133, 145, 235
Circle of Romance; 28, 117, 129, 206, 235
Clarity; 69
Color Intensity, general; 133–136, 140–141, 145, 221, 237
    Depleted; 146–148
    Mottling; 147–148, 177, 188
Combining Indicators; 215
Communication Gap; 185–187, 241–242
Corners; 35–36, 38, 47, 50, 64, 85–86, 91–99, 102–105, 107–108, 153, 198, 208, 221–222, 235–236, 239
Creativity; 205–208
Cupid's Bow; 25, 28–29, 48, 76, 111–113, 115, 123–125, 183–184, 221–223, 236

D
Dancing Lip Prints; 208, 209, 210, 236
Distraction, Lines of; 168, 172
Droopy Lips; 107, 236

E
Energetic Bodies; 134, 136, 140–142, 227, 236, 238
Energized; 82, 104, 132, 141, 157, 159, 207, 236

F
Fading; 135, 141, 145–146, 148–150, 154, 177–180, 183–185, 206
    Apex of the Lip; 183–185
    Hug Pucker (Communication Gap); 185
    Corners (Blinders); 105–106
Fullness; 16, 18, 23, 25, 28, 37, 71–72, 74–80, 114, 117, 130, 222, 236, 239

G
Gale Marks; 172–174, 221
    in the Gourmet Lip Split; 174–175
Gourmet Lip Split; 28, 103, 117, 129–132, 155, 174, 206, 215, 222, 226, 235, 236

H
Hand of God; 193–194
Happy Lips; 107
Helping Hands; 198, 222, 236
Hug Pucker; 25, 28, 75, 117–121, 132, 135, 161, 165, 178, 185–186, 206, 235–237
Hybrid Lip Print; 50, 66–67, 237

I
Indicator; 7, 9, 18–19, 23, 25–29, 35–36, 38, 43, 46, 66, 75–76, 101, 105, 109, 115–117, 121, 123–124, 126–129, 131–135, 221–224, 226, 235–237
Information Eddy; 101–102, 221–222, 237
Information Funnels; 98, 101, 207, 215, 237
Inner Reserves; 150–152
Intuitive Mist; 202, 203, 237
Irregular Lip Print; 61–62, 64–66, 206, 237

J
Jilly Eddy; 5, 7, 18–19, 50, 101, 139, 159, 172, 188, 192, 231, 235, 237
Journey Line; 180, 182, 189, 190, 237

K
KC Miller; 5, 59, 191, 193
Kiss Card; 21–22, 28, 30, 45, 64, 69, 81, 83, 88–89, 104, 133–134, 140, 148, 196, 206–209, 237–238

L
Lines of Concern; 167–168, 222, 237
Lines of Intuition; 194–196, 222, 237
Lip Anatomy Map; 154
Lower Cupid's Bow; 123–125, 222–223, 237

Lower Hug Pucker; 132, 206, 238
Luminous Being; 141, 215, 232, 238

M

Map of the Lips; 35
Mental Memos; 159, 161, 165, 167, 182, 223, 225, 238
    in the Hug Pucker; 161
Mentor; 54–58, 60, 64
Missing Parts; 65, 140, 145, 152–155
Missouri Lip Print; 86, 238
Mother Hen; 121–122, 128, 238
Mother Nature Lines; 194–195, 222, 237
Mottling; 147–148, 177, 188
Multiple Gourmet Lip Split; 131–132

O

Overwhelm, Line of; 189–190

P

Passion; 5, 19, 41, 60, 66, 74, 100, 129–131, 141, 205–206, 215, 236
People Movers; 112, 115–116, 183, 223, 238
Peppering; 145, 151, 166, 223
    Upper Peppering; 151, 166
    Lower Peppering; 151
Personal Pusher; 125–126, 223, 238
Personal Utilities; 141, 238
Physiognomy; 17–18, 238
Pointed Bottom; 126, 238
Position; 81–83, 238
Problem Solver; 40, 50–54, 63–64, 67, 103, 113, 224
Provider; 46–50, 55, 67
Psychic Wedge; 25, 195–198, 238

R

Regret, Lines of; 142, 167–168, 170–172, 182, 222, 225, 237
Role Model; 58–59, 67
Round Bottom; 127

S

Secrets; 35, 91, 104
Seeds of Transformation; 199, 200, 215, 223, 237, 238

Shapes; 29, 43–45, 68, 215, 238
    Diamond; 58–60
    Hybrid; 66–67
    Irregular; 61–66
    Round and Oval; 46–50
    Square and Rectangle, Rectangular; 50–54
    Triangle, Triangular; 54–57
Size; 25, 37, 239
Smooth Top; 113–115, 183
Spacing; 29, 85–89, 91–96, 215, 239
    Corners; 91–96
Spiritual Receptors; 35, 191, 196
Starburst; 200–203, 215, 224, 239
Symbols; 211–213

T
Tipsy Lips; 188, 210, 239
Trauma, Traumatic; 64–66, 128, 153–156, 237

W
White Noise; 161–162
Worry Lines; 168–170
    in the Gourmet Lip Split; 174–175

Z
Zingers; 25, 47, 102–103, 127, 186, 198, 222, 224, 226, 237, 239